For Penny

THE SUMMER OF A DORMOUSE

The Summer of a Dormouse is a vivid testimony to the pleasures and pains of old age. In it we follow John Mortimer—novelist, playwright, erstwhile barrister, and scorge of both Tories and New Labour—through a gloriously full year. This involves working with Franco Zeffirelli, raising money to rebuild the Royal Court Theatre, chairing a committee to advise on who or what will go on the empty plinth in Trafalgar Square, and lunching with old lags in Wormnwood Scrubs. Yet there is no holding back the tide of physical afflictions that come at Sir John through the year. His father takes most of the blame—from him he inherited bronchial asthma, glaucoma and a tendency for his retinas to become detached—but sex and flowers share the responsibility too. Between them they account for a couple of falls that necessitate the occasional use of a wheeelchair and strategies of almost military proportions to cross a room. Public and private, poignant and frank, but above all wonderfully funny, this is John Mortimer at his best.

THE SUMMER OF A DORMOUSE

John Mortimer

CHIVERS PRESS
BATH

First published 2000
by
Viking
This Large Print edition published by
Chivers Press
by arrangement with
Viking
2001

ISBN 0 7540 1598 X

Excerpt from '*The Arrest of Oscar Wilde at the
Cadogan Hotel*' by John Betjeman printed by
permission of John Murray (Publishers) Ltd.
Excerpt from '*As I walked Out One Evening*' by
W.H. Auden printed by permission of Faber
and Faber Limited.

British Library Cataloguing in Publication Data available

'When one subtracts from life infancy (which is vegetation), sleep, eating and swilling, buttoning and unbuttoning—how much remains of downright existence? The summer of a dormouse.'

Byron, *Journals*

'They say the seeds of what we will do are in all of us, but it always seemed to me that in those who make jokes in life the seeds are covered with better soil and with a higher grade of manure.'

Ernest Hemingway, *A Moveable Feast*

CHAPTER ONE

The time will come in your life, it will almost certainly come, when the voice of God will thunder at you from a cloud, 'From this day forth thou shalt not be able to put on thine own socks.'

To the young, to the middle aged, even, this may seem a remote and improbable accident that only happens to other people. It has to be said, however, that the day will most probably dawn when your pale foot will wander through the air, incapable of hitting the narrow opening of a suspended sock. Those fortunate enough to live with families will call out for help. The situation is, in minor ways, humiliating and comical.

It's a law of script writing that scenes get shorter and the action speeds up towards the end. In childhood, the afternoons spread out for years. For the old, the years flicker past like the briefest of afternoons. The playwright Christopher Fry, now ninety-three, told me that after the age of eighty you seem to be having breakfast every five minutes. These film scenes, building to an inevitable climax, tend less to tragedy than farce. Dying is a matter of slapstick and prat falls. The ageing process is not gradual or gentle. It rushes up, pushes you over and runs off laughing. No one

1

should grow old who isn't ready to appear ridiculous.

*   *   *

Flowers, sex and my father have been responsible for my disabilities.

So far as the sex was concerned, it, or rather the lack of it, was not my immediate concern. A close friend rang at the door of my flat in London, her purpose being to come in and discuss the mysterious failure of the man she lived with to make love to her on anything like a regular basis. Skipping eagerly down a steep flight of stairs to open the door to this tale of distress, I had my first fall, causing me to have to defend a footman, who had assisted a multi-murdering butler in the killing of yet another of his employers, with my leg in a plaster cast. Then an Achilles tendon failed me, not snapping dramatically in a hard game of tennis (when the doctor asked me if I became breathless when taking exercise I had to plead ignorance, as I have never taken exercise), but simply sagging and giving up in despair. As a result of an operation to rejuvenate it my other leg swelled up like a balloon, contracting a thrombosis.

Then the flowers took over. I fell from the top of a terrace in the garden whilst cutting dead heads off the dahlias, causing an ulcerated leg which hasn't healed for two

2

years. Later, buying red-hot pokers in a Maida Vale garden centre, I crashed down the lavatory steps and ripped knee muscles. All over the world, men and women who have experienced a reasonable quantity of life are toppling over, collapsing in kitchens or hurtling down stairs.

From my father I inherited bronchial asthma, glaucoma and a tendency for my retinas to become displaced. He also left me, in the house he built, a number of walking sticks.

Although he was blind these were never white; that would have been a demand for sympathy. They are solid sticks of clouded malacca, with crooked handles and large rubber tips which cling reassuringly to the ground, and when wedged between bricks or paving stones they provide solid support. These sticks dangle from door handles, cupboard tops and window-sills, frequently forgotten. I grab one and hobble out into the garden. The red-hot pokers, I'm glad to see, are not doing particularly well.

*   *   *

Partial immobility, clearly a disadvantage for mountaineers, professional runners or stars of the ballet, has fewer terrors for writers. The writer lives in a sedentary state, his blood freezing, his hands and feet growing as cold in

3

the hottest summer as in winter time, turning up the heating so that active, non-writing companions complain, tear off their clothes and swelter.

The writer also lives in a world free of time, able to dive back into the past, foretell the future or capture the single moment of composition. Hemingway, in *A Moveable Feast*, describes the thin sliver of wood emerging from the pencil sharpener as he prepares to construct a sentence over a glass of cold beer in a Paris café. He sits and awaits events. In time they are bound to come to him.

*   *   *

I'm at home in the country when I'm summoned to meet Franco Zeffirelli at the Athenaeum Hotel. Ever available, I make a date.

'Darling, I rely on you. You are my last and only hope. I ask you to save my life, the life that is precious to me. Only you can do it. I feel that most strongly. Only you in the whole world!'

I have had mild flirtations with Franco before, but they have come, like unsatisfactory love affairs, to nothing. This time it is the full seduction. Franco has grown paler, plumper, and the good looks which made him a beautiful young man, discovered and favoured by Visconti, have somewhat disintegrated, but his charm is undimmed. He is exhausted by an

4

overnight flight from the Met in New York, and he has stopped off on his way home to Rome.

He has designed the sets for and is about to direct a production of *Aïda* which will open a great new opera house in Tokyo. He is the greatest living opera director—ask him where Tosca should set the candles by Scarpia's corpse and he will tell you that the exact position has been decided by Puccini's music. He is wearing a blouson and the thick woollen tights favoured by ballet dancers. One pale hand holds a tumbler of whisky, qualified by lumps of ice, and the other a long, thin cigarette. Chain-smoking these fags, he tells me, would be an infallible cure for the asthma which plagues me. He orders coffee and toast, flirts a little with the Italian waiter and explains his film to me. It is, in the loosest possible way, a fragment of his autobiography.

I have become fond of Franco and feel a sort of affinity with him as we were born in the same year, five years after the end of the First World War and sixteen years before the start of the Second. I entered the world in Hampstead, the only child of a divorce barrister and a one-time art teacher. Franco was the single, illegitimate child of a dressmaker in Florence. His absentee father had amassed, during the 1914 war when most husbands were away fighting, a huge number of mistresses. I think the reason why Franco, as an Italian Senator, is so opposed to abortion, is that if his mother had taken that course, the world would have been deprived of the best production of *Tosca*.

After his mother's early death, he was looked after by an Irish secretary who worked in his father's office. She taught him about Shakespeare and Elizabeth Barrett Browning. Interest was also taken in him by his mother's ex-customers, the English ladies, nicknamed the *'Scorpione'* by the local inhabitants, who lived in Florence for the culture, or because it was cheaper than England, or because no one wanted them at home. In the 1930s these ladies admired Mussolini, who made the trains run on time and who, it seems, had offered them protection when and if Italy entered the war. So his film is called *Tea with Mussolini.*

Franco was pressed into a Young Fascist organization, but when the war started he avoided the army and joined the Resistance. One of the best scenes in his story, later cut because it would all have had to be played in Italian, concerns his capture by the Fascists. A young Fascist puts a gun down Franco's trousers and offers to shoot off his virility if he doesn't betray members of the Italian Underground. He also asks for Franco's address and the name of his father. When these particulars are given the Fascist looks severely shaken and withdraws the threatening gun. It turns out that he, also, is a bastard son

6

of the same promiscuous father: so he sets his half-brother free. Later Franco's father says, 'You blame me for having had so many mistresses; but if I hadn't you'd be dead now, or at least impotent.' I don't know how true the story is, but the film sadly misses it.

What is certainly true is that Franco met up with the Scots Greys as they fought their way up Italy, and joined them as a young interpreter. He went recently to a reunion dinner in Aberdeen, where elderly sergeants called out, 'How are you, Franco?' and greeted him like a long lost friend.

As this is his story, Franco feels particularly sensitive and protective about it. The table in his suite is piled high with scripts, the work of talented and well-known writers who have failed to meet the requirements of Franco's memory. The film must, to some extent, mirror his past, although it seems to include fictional variations. Luca, the film version of Franco as a child and teenager, is, for instance, to show marked heterosexual tendencies. I will also be allowed to invent the English ladies and create a new band of *Scorpione*, but Franco as a child has to remain irresistibly virtuous.

After I have promised to think it over and write a short treatment, we go down to lunch with the Italian producers. Signora Zanoni is small, energetic and unfailingly optimistic. Doctor Tosti is elegant and world weary, as

7

befits a man accustomed to dealing with the inner workings of Italian television. Franco, his whisky glass refilled, says he rarely eats lunch, and then tucks into a large plate of pasta. We raise our glasses to 'a beautiful film, darling', coupled with success to the *Scorpione* and the child Luca.

*   *   *

I have sent off a treatment to Franco and I am waiting for his reaction. I am at home once again, with the producer Adrian Bate, discussing the filming of *Cider with Rosie* in Laurie Lee's Gloucestershire countryside. Our three dogs are barking at intruders and when I look through the window of my writing room I see a blonde woman leaning over the gate. I call, telling her the dogs aren't nearly as vicious as they sound. She turns out to be Pat York, a good photographer, over from Los Angeles. When I let her in, she has an immediate request. 'Would you mind taking off all your clothes?'

It's eleven o'clock in the morning. Adrian and I are drinking coffee, discussing casting and harming nobody. What, I wonder, is Mrs York after? 'I'm not very keen on the idea,' I say. 'I mean, *why* exactly?'

'I'm going to have an exhibition. Photographs of naked people and corpses. It will only be seen in St Petersburg, so you needn't worry. You'll find it a truly significant experience. Just take a look at these!'

She shows me a large photograph of her plumber, stark naked as he mends the waste-disposal unit in the kitchen of the Yorks' Los Angeles home. The man is in a curious attitude, bent backwards to expose a full frontal view, with only his head concealed beneath the sink. This picture is accompanied by a letter from the plumber testifying to the fact that being photographed naked under the kitchen sink by Mrs York was undoubtedly the most profound and moving moment of his life. There is another photograph, this time of her husband's unclothed agent answering the telephone and apparently enjoying an equally liberating experience.

'I'll do almost anything for you,' I tell her, 'except be photographed with my clothes off. Who, anyway, would want a naked septuagenarian with an unhealed leg in an exhibition, even if it will only be shown in St Petersburg? And I don't want to be included among the corpses.'

Mrs York shrugs, admits defeat, and asks Adrian Bate if he has any objection to taking off his clothes. She gets an equally firm refusal. Then my wife comes in. Penny is a woman who apparently knows no fear. She has hunted in Ireland, where the horses jump over barbed wire or scramble up walls and land on piles of rocks. She has swum with sharks and laughed

9

at death threats from hunt saboteurs. Brought up on a pig farm, she knows many animals are born to be eaten, and that most people will naturally end up with their clothes off. She sees no objection to being photographed undressed and is reassured when she hears she will only be on view in St Petersburg. The remaining question is where the picture should be set. I suggest some suitably rural scene, such as her feeding the chickens.

So, dressed only in a pair of wellington boots and carrying a bucketful of scraps, Penny enters the chicken run. When Mrs York has finished snapping she goes down the hill to the house of a fearless interviewer of celebrities and scourge of political humbugs. The star who asked the then Home Secretary the same question fourteen times, in a bruising attempt to get a simple answer, refuses to take off a stitch of clothing. Elizabeth, the mother of his children, has no such inhibitions and strips for the camera as readily as Penny, to be beautifully photographed with a twin baby on each elegant tit. I don't know what any of this proves, except that when it comes to courage, women win over men every time.

The next morning my agent Anthony Jones, well known for his brief and often ironic telephone calls, rings and says, 'Bad news, I'm afraid. Franco wants you to write the script. He also invites you to stay at his house in Rome.'

CHAPTER TWO

To check an article my daughter Emily has written, I'm looking for *Titus Andronicus* and the details of the injuries inflicted on the fragile Lavinia after her rape (her hands were cut off and her tongue torn out to prevent her giving evidence, a scene which shows that Shakespeare was lucky to have died before the birth of the Broadcasting Standards Committee, or the advent of the Film Censor). I lug the big, red volume of collected plays off the shelf and it happens to fall open at *Henry VI, Part Two*, Act III, scene one. For some reason I read only the last two lines of the second column at the foot of the page:

> This devil here shall be my substitute,
> For that John Mortimer, which now is dead.

The room, unendurably stifling to the rest of my family, turns cold. *'That John Mortimer . . .'* Could it be the John Mortimer who attracted the attention of a future Archbishop at Oxford, who defended the *Oz* editors and was, in his seventy-sixth year, mugged by a baby, who has now turned up his toes, handed in his chips, dropped finally off the twig? Is there a terrible warning in the chance opening of a book? I turn the page hurriedly and pass on to

Titus Andronicus in search of light relief. Having resolutely avoided check-ups (from fear of what they might discover), I have never had a doctor pronounce a sentence of death after a fixed term of years, but I can imagine that such a grim verdict might almost come as a relief, adding a magical value to the years remaining. And, although my death is only announced by a quotation, I find it, in a single cold moment, strangely stimulating.

After reading *Titus Andronicus* for a while I go back to the lines in *Henry VI, Part Two*. They are spoken by the Duke of York, who is manipulating the 'devil', a stubborn man from Ashford named John Cade who, with York's help, organized a surprisingly successful rebellion, using my name. After his capture a pardon was made out to him in the name of John Mortimer, which was found not to be his real name, so Cade was executed. Therefore the open book doesn't announce my death; merely the unhappy end of a pseudonym.

The fear of death may leave many mortals chilled and trembling, but it apparently had no such effect on Lord Runcie, one of the few former Archbishops of Canterbury to have kept pigs and fought in the artillery. I was at Oxford early in the war and, despite the austerity, there were still echoes of *Brideshead Revisited* lingering in the corners of Christchurch quadrangles. There was an aesthete who lay naked on a sofa listening to a hugely amplified record of the Verdi *Requiem*, which shook the arch of Peckwater after midnight. There was an eccentric, later distinguished, historian who regularly fell drunk into Mercury, a small but inviting pool. You could still get lunch, or tea with anchovy toast and honey buns, brought over to your rooms. I lived in Meadow Building, as did the young Runcie. In his biography he speaks of asking our scout Bustyn why John Mortimer wore purple corduroy trousers and was always having young women to tea. To this our scout is alleged to have replied, 'Mr Mortimer, sir, has an irrepressible member.' This is not the way one would wish to be spoken about in the life of an Archbishop of Canterbury.

Now, it seems, this gentle and admired cleric is facing death. His daughter-in-law says he sits at a family luncheon smiling happily and saying how much he is looking forward to dying so that he can meet Basil Hume, the deceased Cardinal, and so many friends. His grandchildren, who love him, are upset and ask him not to die, but he looks forward, with smiling certainty, to an interdenominational encounter beyond the grave. A belief in the afterlife, many people would say, is a great comfort to us at the end of our lives; but probably not to the grandchildren.

Or is it? The anticipation of heaven was also accompanied by the fear of hell, of which Dr Johnson lived in perpetual terror. Religious

13

judges, after a lifetime of trying others, look forward apprehensively to an appearance in the dock of some celestial Central Criminal Court, with God as the Lord Chief Justice. Lord Hailsham, when Lord Chancellor, confessed that he had done wrongs and intended to plead guilty and throw himself on the mercy of the court. When I asked him the precise nature of these wrongs, he muttered, 'Private matters' and played with his paper clips. No doubt it would be both pleasant and interesting to chat with Cardinal Hume, but would you want to do so for all eternity?

My father, unlike Archbishop Runcie, was not keen on the idea of the soul's immortality. He thought it was a remarkably boring concept, like living for all eternity in some vast transcendental hotel with absolutely nothing to do in the evenings. And yet, I comfort myself, he has his immortality. He lives in my memory and I think of him daily, as though he were living here in the house he built in the country and I was away in London, or Los Angeles, or some such improbable place. I can find great quantities of him in my children, in their laughter at serious moments and in their relish for words. Is this the only immortality we can believe in? Come to think of it, there is a downside. Traces of Judge Jeffreys, Torquemada and Jack the Ripper, not to mention Dr Goebbels, Ceaucescu and Attila the Hun may still be at large and strolling round the world.

Most of life is spent without a thought of death, and those who die young must be quite unprepared for the performance of dying. Now I wonder exactly how to play it, and how long the certainty of its arrival lasts. Is there a time for a lengthy and considered farewell, or do you have to grab a moment for a few memorable last words? For how long had Charles the Second made up his mind to apologize for being an 'unconscionable time a'dying', and would death have cheated him if it had taken him suddenly while he was feeding the spaniels or making love to Nell Gwynne? Would he have gasped out hurriedly, 'I've been an unconscionable time . . .' and never been able to finish the sentence?

During the recent trial of a war criminal at the Old Bailey, there was an argument about its reporting in the *Daily Mirror*, which might have amounted to contempt. The problem was solved more or less amicably and that night one of the prosecuting barristers went to see his father, who was seriously ill in the London Clinic, and told him about the troublesome report. The father, a distinguished politician, sat up in bed, said, 'Bloody *Daily Mirror* again!' and promptly died. Whether or not they were justified, I don't think anyone would choose these for his last words. The last thing I remember *my* father saying was, 'I'm always angry when I'm dying,' and I don't know if that

15

was a sentence long rehearsed or the inspiration of the final moment.

'Here it comes at last, the Distinguished Thing,' was what Henry James said when he felt that death was not far away. In spite of the opportunity for effective last words, it must be worse if the Distinguished Thing announces its imminent arrival and then dawdles for six months or a year.

*   *   *

I am on my way to Franco's house, sitting on an aeroplane and vaguely anxious. Will there be a wheelchair to meet me at Rome airport? Sitting in such a chair at parties, your eyes are at the level of speechless crotches. Drinks are held, samosas and cocktail sausages nibbled and gobbled high above your head. You are a child again because no one stoops to have a conversation with you. There is laughter, gossip, flirtation in the upper air. In the world of childhood and old age there is isolation among the knees, only an occasional face is lowered, offers a samosa or a scrap of smoked salmon on soggy bread, and floats up again to the grown-up world.

If wheelchair riders are third-class citizens at parties, they are upgraded at airports, moving in triumph past long queues at passport control, getting only a polite pat at the search for weapons, being let on to the

16

empty plane first with children travelling alone and other cripples. Claiming a wheelchair on account of the leg and a blind eye has improved my experience of airports 100 per cent. I have been pushed by retired businessmen eking out their pensions, students in their gap year or, occasionally, beautiful girls in uniform. Only once did the wheelchair experience turn from a privileged ride to a journey into hell.

It was at Milan airport and I was waiting at the check-in desk for the athletic beauty who had zipped me past queues on my arrival to take me to the aeroplane for home. It was clearly her day off and her place was taken by a malign dwarf, a small and sinister chair-pusher who offered me, with a shrug of contempt, a chair clearly designed for a child. Wedged into it, with my knees pressing against my ears, I was hurtled through the crowds towards a distant room, bleak, airless and windowless, in which a line of wheelchairs, parked against a blank wall, contained the partially paralysed and the terminally ill being taken away, perhaps, to die in Palermo. Finding a parking spot at the end of this line, my wheelchair Quasimodo put on the brakes and dumped me.

Gasping for air, I struggled to my feet and limped to a bar for a reviving Prosecco. As I drank I heard a final call for the flight to Heathrow. I rejoined the parade of lost souls and at last Quasimodo reappeared and sped me at a kind of uneven gallop to the gate at which the glass doors were now closed. I could see, however, the BA plane on the tarmac, so I struggled to my feet again, only to be pulled back by my driver, who said, 'You can't move. You're blind! Wait for the lorry!'

Then I saw, far away on the other side of the airport, a lorry with a huge crane on its back. It was advancing slowly, remorselessly towards the glass doors. I'm still trying to forget being pushed on to a platform, being hoisted into the air by the giant crane and delivered like a piece of excess baggage at the doorway of the aircraft, to the fascinated amusement of the returning tourists. I'd rather have been at knee level, bored to tears at a drinks party.

* * *

'I don't really like this house. It's very cold and dark and it smells of old dogs.'

Franco's driver, gardener and friend, a beefy, quietly spoken man whose leisure hours are spent watching television, had decanted me from an airport wheelchair into the back of a Mercedes. We listened to a deafening football commentary all the way to Cinecitta, the area of large houses built for stars around the studios during the past flowering of the Italian film industry. We stopped at a pair of forbidding gates, shrouded by dark trees, which swung open at a coded message. Now I am in the house I'd criticized in a whispered call home from the telephone in the hall.

In the surrounding shadows a number of men, both young and old, are lurking. There are also no less than six Jack Russells, loved by their master, who have a tendency to mount the dinner table and eat the spaghetti. The prevailing gloom is relieved by bright flowers and naked statues. The furniture is loaded with silver-framed photographs of Franco with various heads of state, highly placed clerics and opera singers. The kitchen is full of the elderly servants and neighbours whom Franco generously supports. One of them, a small prop man of uncertain age, is often there cooking his own meals. Like most Roman houses it is unprotected from the damp and cold which persist for much of the year. If you turn on more than one bar of the electric fire, the lights go out. The problem seems to be that, unlike Franco's more palatial house in Positano, this one belongs not to him but to a landlord, so neither party is prepared to undertake any improvements; in the garden, the plants are in pots to be ready for swift removal.

Writing for the movies, I've found, leads to varying degrees of imprisonment. I have been press-ganged on to a large yacht, which weighed anchor during the night and steamed off to an unknown destination to prevent my escape. I have been shut up in soulless offices and hotel bedrooms—one director turned the photographs of my family to face the wall, making sure I concentrated on the script. On this occasion, Penny had given me the number of a friend, Molly, who worked for an English newspaper in Rome. Molly, it seemed, was engaged in a love affair with a Dutch priest who held some important post in the Vatican. They would, my wife was sure, be delighted to go out to dinner with me whenever I wanted. Under house arrest with Franco, I insist on evening parole.

Dead on time a battered Fiat Uno rattles through the electronic gates, driven by Father Erik, wearing a T-shirt, an anorak and jeans. In the back of the car, smiling a welcome, is a black-haired, blue-eyed Irish journalist. As we leave Casa Zeffirelli, I ask Father Erik how he and Molly got to know each other.

'We met at a discussion group.' Father Erik seems to look back at a happy memory.

'Really? What did you discuss at this discussion group?'

'Oh, questions such as "Whither Europe?", "The Future of Africa" and "Third World Debt".'

'Piss off!' Molly laughs at him from the back of the Fiat. 'It was Alcoholics Anonymous!'

During the ten days I am in Rome we have dinner together every night. In a better and more appropriate tribute to the millennium than ours, Rome has restored and repaired its churches. Santa Maria in the Trastevere, with its golden façade, glows like a jewel in the dark city. We drive round the Castel Sant'Angelo, where Tosca jumped to her death, past the wedding-cake monument to Victor Emmanuel and along the banks of the Tiber. We dine in the Jewish quarter, near the Trevi Fountain, and in the Trastevere square, in small, cheap restaurants with bare floors, fresh anchovies and plate-sized mushrooms and bollito misto with salsa verde. I order Sambucca and, when it is well alight, discuss the possibility, at some future date, of women priests and married clerics in the Vatican. Molly dreads the possibility of Father Erik being promoted to a post of such importance that, to avoid all risk of scandal, sex would have to be off the menu. He is a priest who has travelled much and worked hard for the poor and politically oppressed. He and Molly are simply two excellent people who are very much in love.

CHAPTER THREE

The world's not always unkind and cries for help are frequently answered. I have broadcast the dreaded sentence of the Almighty with regard to the putting on of the socks. There now arrives a huge package by special delivery from New Zealand. I start to open it eagerly, cutting and tearing at sealed wrapping paper and boxes within boxes. At last I unearth a mysterious object, shrouded in bubble wrap. More ripping reveals a gigantic leg, from below the knee to the toes, fashioned out of heavy wire coated in white plastic, having the look of some exhibit in a museum of torture. With it there's a letter telling me that it comes with the compliments of a couple in New Zealand who, having heard of my problem, have invented the 'Soxon' and had it constructed to their specifications. A largish sock is to be inserted into the top and the leg lowered into the depths of the cage. Unhappily, having few mechanical skills, I find the leg, once in, difficult to extricate. Even a sockless day seems preferable to clumping round with one foot caged in a strange device. So I continue to rely on friends, and the wonderful sock-putting-on machine stands in a corner as a tribute to human ingenuity and kindness.

*　　　*　　　*

'We're going to be marvellously happy. Oh, Laurie. A little cottage and a grammy and each other.' So wrote a lovesick girl—most of the girls in the Gloucestershire village of Slad were in love with Laurie Lee. But the girl, the cottage and the gramophone (of the wind-up variety) weren't enough for him. Son of an eccentric, highly strung, porcelain beauty of a mother—she had worked as a maid in a grand house—and an absentee father, he 'walked out one midsummer morning' to a new life as the lover of many beautiful, and some wealthy, women, and to be one of the literary stars of his generation. When Laurie Lee's poetry was published in *Horizon*, Stephen Spender assured him they didn't only buy it because of Laurie's 'proletarian origins'. In *Cider with Rosie* he produced a hugely successful account of his childhood, a rural idyll which became required reading for generations of urban schoolchildren.

I first encountered the Lee magic during the war, when we both worked for a government film unit called the 'Crown' in Pinewood Studios. He wasn't particularly happy there and played his violin sadly in the corridors, remembering his days in Spain, where he had found the war far more romantic than England in the Blitz. We were in love with the same doe-eyed girl, Mavis from the production office, and Laurie's soft Gloucestershire accent and floppy forelock gave him a distinct advantage in the race for her affection. He was a good friend to me, in spite of our rivalry over Mavis, and when he could stand the film business no longer and left, he bequeathed me his job. From then on I had the words 'Script

23

Writer' emblazoned on my battledress and I learned the basic rules of film-making, which led me, in the course of time, into the shadowy recesses of Franco's house.

Now I have done a television film adaptation of *Cider with Rosie*. The book is beautifully written and, together with lyric descriptions of landscapes and love, doesn't try to hide the poverty, loneliness and suffering of rural life at the end of the First World War. Doubts have been raised, as they have of Laurie's writing about the Spanish Civil War, about its accuracy. The book may have its fictional moments, but it still tells a poetic truth about English country life. He had read it all on tape, so his voice as an old man can be used as a commentary to the film, although Laurie died just before we started work.

I sit in the Slad pub with Kathy, whom Laurie had met when she was a child, and encountered again as a 'shapely, light-limbed, flat-bellied young beauty'. Later she went on holiday to Italy, ate a good deal of spaghetti and put on weight. On her return, Laurie said he couldn't marry her if she was more than twelve stone and he weighed her. Happily she tipped the scales at eleven stone twelve pounds and their marriage lasted for the rest of his life. Kathy thinks he'd have been glad I was doing the script, and I am anxious to repay him for giving me his job.

*   *   *

Writing film scripts is like sending soldiers over the top in the First World War. Very few of them come back alive. For a long time it seems that *Tea with Mussolini* has gone missing, believed killed. *Cider with Rosie*, however, is alive and well, and I set out to visit the location, mainly for the pleasure of seeing my daughter Emily, who is playing Miss Flynn, a dotty character of dubious reputation who finally drowns herself in the village pond.

Unless you are actively engaged in the production, seeing a film being made has all the excitement of watching paint dry, or waiting for a yew hedge to grow. For this reason it's often said that anyone who manages to stay awake can direct a film. One great Hollywood director couldn't quite manage it. He was to be seen, quite often, fast asleep in his own shot.

The Stage is a valuable periodical which advertises jobs, tells you what's going on in all the provincial theatres and, almost always, publishes favourable notices which, being given out with universal generosity, don't carry much weight when they are quoted. Hence the well-known theatrical saying, 'What are the three most useless things in the world? A man's nipples, the Pope's balls and a good notice in *The Stage*.' To these three may be added: a writer on a film set. If you want to

25

hear your dialogue repeated over and over again during ten takes; if you want to wait while proceedings are delayed by aeroplanes, or flies in the gate, or a microphone with performing ambitions which steals into the shot; if you want to find you're standing on a cable or, like that old Hollywood director, going to sleep in the BG of someone's POV, then dash off to a location. A writer on a film set has no function except to eat the catering, relieve himself in the 'honeywagon' and chat up the extras. These extras, coolly treated and indifferently paid, live for the constant food breaks, the cooked breakfast, elevenses, lunch and tea, served from the catering wagon and eaten, usually, in the bus. If a break for any meal is announced, the extras set off from a flying start and always head the queue to load their plates.

One director was making, the story goes, a film about motor racing. The extras singularly failed to register surprise, terror and sorrow at the disastrous events in the script. Faced with the camera, they looked, despite the assistant director's yelled instructions, uninterested and unconcerned. There was only one course for the director to take. He ordered the props man to put a charge of dynamite in the catering wagon and then announced a tea break. As usual, the extras set off for their goal at a smart and hungry trot. And then the catering wagon blew up and they were showered with sandwiches, jam doughnuts, sticky buns and dark cake. The expressions of horror and tragic loss on their faces were then just right.

It's worth an occasional visit to the set, however, to keep up with the language, to meet those middle-aged, even elderly technicians known as the 'gaffer' and the 'best boy' and to hear the lighting cameraman give the order to 'Kill that baby.' 'Babies' are, of course, lights, which can also be 'pups', 'blondes' or 'redheads'. So there may be calls to 'lose the pup' or 'give me two blondes and three redheads'. Any piece of furniture or equipment found missing on a film set is said to be 'travelling'.

In the scene I watch, Emily is dressed as a pre-Raphaelite villager singing snatches of song and throwing twigs and dead leaves on to a small bonfire. I am puzzled when the first assistant calls on the prop man to 'Put a bit of petrol on Mr Kingsley.' The prop man obliges and the dying bonfire is stung into a blaze. Then there is a new set-up and the first assistant gives further instructions. 'Please move Mr Kingsley across the garden. We want Ben to smoke into the shot.' 'Why,' I ask, 'are bonfires in films called Ben Kingsley?' I should, of course, have known the answer. Ben Kingsley played Gandhi and Gandhi was burnt on a funeral pyre.

Someone on the set worked on the film in

which Gandhi, Ben Kingsley and bonfires became synonymous. They were shooting Gandhi's funeral, he tells me, Indian extras filled the landscape, the pyre was lit, Dickie Attenborough was surveying the whole tragic scene from a crane or some such position of directorial eminence, and the first assistant shouted over the tannoy, his voice echoing across the landscape, 'Quiet please! Gandhi's dead! Look sad! Turn over!'

*　　　*　　　*

No more news from Rome since I sent off the first draft of Franco's script. It's spring in the country, the best time of the year, with the azaleas out and sheets of butter-coloured daffodils, first planted when the house was built, in the shadows round the copse. I'm going to London as little as possible, but I have to today because there's a meeting at the Royal Court Theatre to discuss an important subject—thrush.

Like Savonarola preaching at a Florentine orgy, the Royal Court stared down the King's Road in the swinging and irresponsible sixties. The theatre had not always taken itself so seriously. In the distant past it had been financed by an impresario who, in the days when naked women were not allowed to move on the stage, invented a system of turntables on which their beauty could be seen from all angles. But early in the last century it became the home of Shaw, Granville Barker and John Osborne, a place where the British middle classes could fill the stalls and thoroughly enjoy having their country, their prejudices and, indeed, their whole way of life brilliantly rubbished.

I've never had a play done at the Court, or had much to do with the theatre, until I was invited to become its Chairman, and I accepted with enthusiasm. The artistic director, Max Stafford-Clark, had run the Court for a long time, directing brilliantly and putting on plays by a new generation of Sloane Square writers, such as Caryl Churchill and Timberlake Wertenbaker. I suppose Max would be classed among the Puritans; he was religiously devoted to the high principles of the Court. Only writers, and never actors, were allowed to have their names in lights on the front of the theatre. The sets tended towards greyness, the entertainment designed to be thoughtful rather than visual.

Together with its great traditions and achievements, the Court had various defects. The wooden posts underpinning the stage were rotting and dangerous. The machinery flying the scenery was also a hazard. The dressing-rooms were a disgrace to a so-called civilized society. The roof leaked—a bucket on the side of the stage received the drips in severe weather, and the noise from Sloane

Square Underground Station was so persistent that I heard that Harold Pinter had asked for the trains to be stopped during his technical rehearsal. The staff were loyal, hard working and poorly paid.

Soon after my arrival, I saw a play set in a Caribbean country and the cast included a number of live chickens. After the show, I asked the front-of-house manager how things were going. 'Not too well,' she said, and I thought she added, 'One of the hands died.' A hand? What could that mean? Some pale, undernourished girl, I thought, some poverty stricken Assistant Stage Manager, exhausted by all-night get-ins and prolonged dress rehearsals.

'Good heavens, how terrible! Where did she die?'

'In her hutch, up on the roof of the theatre.'

Things at the Court were even worse than I feared. Was there some shack, some temporary outbuilding on the roof where theatre workers who couldn't afford rents in Kensington and Chelsea dossed down for the night? There was one more question to ask.

'Have you told the family?'

'We didn't think that was absolutely necessary.' The front-of-house girl was laughing heartily. 'Not with a hen.'

My advancing age, or her particular way with vowels, had led me to believe that the deceased was a person and not a chicken.

*　　*　　*

Max loved the theatre and was often to be seen as the audience arrived for a first night polishing the glass in the street doors with a rag and a bottle of Windolene. His contract had been frequently extended and was up for renewal again. Understandably, he wanted to stay and had many friends and devoted supporters on the theatre's Board. A majority decided, however, that it was time for a change.

Stephen Daldry was running the minute theatre in Notting Hill Gate. In a space not much larger than an average sitting-room, he put on sixteenth-century Spanish plays with huge casts and bewitching scenery. The son of a south-coast bank official, he had joined an Italian circus as a clown—there could probably be no better way of starting a career in the theatre. Possessed of instant and irresistible charm, he has huge theatrical imagination and is somewhat accident prone, often falling off his bike and once into the stage machinery, of which he is particularly fond. He began at the Court with Arnold Wesker's play *The Kitchen*. For this he built a theatre in the round at the level of the dress circle, leaving the stalls in subterranean darkness. Although the number of paying customers was, by this means, reduced, the production worked marvellously.

Then came the Lottery. An excited public poured money into it and money poured out to a number of good causes, which included the rebuilding of theatres but not the putting on of plays. For this reason, there was a serious possibility of the country being full of theatres with luxurious dressing-rooms, splendid showers, glittering bars and smoothly working stage machinery, but no plays. The Lottery could also be criticized as a tax on the poor, who bought tickets on the extremely remote chance of escaping to a better world, but found themselves, instead, paying for the culture and comfort of the well-heeled travellers in society's club class.

However, the Lottery offered a once-in-a-lifetime chance of rebuilding a leaking and dangerous Royal Court. Stephen visited small theatres in Europe and America for examples and warnings. Architects were employed who showed us a beguiling model; the old, well-loved auditorium was set in a brilliant new building, complete with a spacious restaurant underneath Sloane Square, so we would no longer have to entertain arts ministers and visiting stars in a tiny office with a malfunctioning fridge. An enthusiastic theatrical consultant advised us to substitute benches for chairs in the new theatre. 'Benches,' he smiled blissfully, 'lead to thigh contact.' For this reason, he argued, acts of love and the adultery rate in Kilburn had risen steeply since the introduction of benches in a theatre there. Thigh contact, I decided, was all very well, but not if you happened to be sitting next to a hostile and unattractive critic.

So we put in our application and the Royal Court was among the first winners, getting a mouth-watering £21 million. We cheered then, as did Sadlers Wells and Covent Garden, ignorant at the time of what the future might bring.

Not everyone was happy, however. Timberlake Wertenbaker is an important playwright. Brought up by a surrogate mother in the Basque country, while her American journalist parents toured Europe in search of stories, she learned Greek at school, went to university in New York and with *Their Country's Good* and *Three Birds Alighting on a Field* scored two of the major successes of the Max Stafford-Clark regime. She was involved in the thorny question of the proposed seats in the new theatre. The architects, anxious to escape from the old theatrical convention of faded red velvet, had opted for black leather. This was the subject of Timberlake's first major campaign and it was on behalf of women. She had long complained that we didn't do enough plays by women, and that the male-produced plays we did featured men of faddish attitudes. To add insult to injury, we were about to invest in a type of chair (not, I'm glad to say, benches) clearly calculated to give

33

women thrush. I had not heard before of the thrush-producing qualities of black leather, although I also had some doubts about the chairs on the grounds that they might evoke, in some members of the audience, unhappy memories of visits to the dentist. Rows of black leather chairs, when empty in the Festival Hall, looked, in an uncomfortable way I thought, like a Fascist rally. Arguments with the architects, who were keen to order the chairs, occupied a considerable time, until I was persuaded that they should be allowed to complete their conception of the theatre; to decide otherwise would be rather like forcing an author to rewrite his second act. Timberlake was unappeased and stuck to her nightmare vision of female writers and audiences shunning the Royal Court for fear of thrush. What was the solution, apart from providing pots of live yoghurt with the programmes?

After further prolonged debate I decided it was time to bring matters to a head. The seats would be put on trial and each side would call medical evidence. So I'm sitting with the architects and their experts and the Court's Board, eager to be instructed, but, for the moment, no Timberlake appears. We get news that, all thrush forgotten for the moment, she has gone to London airport to research a play. After an interval she arrives alone. The architects' expert tells us that women can contract thrush from any sort of seat and that leather is no more dangerous than faded plush. Timberlake makes an eloquent and impassioned speech and calls for a secret ballot. I appoint Vicki Heywood, the constantly cheerful, ever efficient Executive Director, to be the returning officer. By an almost unanimous vote the new Royal Court has been declared a thrush-free zone with leather seats and a moment of theatrical history has come and gone.

*   *   *

After a long siesta, Franco's film has stirred, stretched and awoken again. A long argument about the completion guarantee has been settled. Cher, a bankable star, has agreed to play the rich American lover of Florentine boys on the make. Most exciting for me is the prospect of Joan Plowright being cast as Franco's errant father's secretary and his boyhood mentor. This calls for a new and, in theory anyway, improved script.

Working on films consists largely of rewriting, a process during which the producer suffers from increasing insecurity and the writer from the danger of terminal boredom setting in. I persuade Franco to come to London and we work in the Athenaeum Hotel with Angela, who was the continuity girl on some of John Huston's greatest pictures.

'They can't say that,' she whispers as Franco dictates some ornate and operatic lines of dialogue, and she kindly taps out my English understatements for the ladies caught up in the war.

At the end of each day, Franco reads the script with delight and says, 'Wonderful, darling. I always knew you would be my salvation.' By next morning, when he has read it again, it has become seriously flawed and we have clearly missed or forgotten the film's most important message. I beg him not to read the script again but to go out and enjoy himself, perhaps have sex.

'No,' he says firmly and without regret. 'I tried that last night and other person was not paying attention.'

* * *

We get a call from Pat York in Los Angeles. She has been in London and left the photographs with the hall porter in a Piccadilly hotel. It was a Sunday, so she couldn't buy an envelope to put them in and cover their nakedness. We make a quick trip to Piccadilly, where we find the hall porter poring over the unforgettable image of Penny, feeding the chickens, wearing nothing but her wellington boots.

CHAPTER FOUR

'Father Erik's been promoted!'

My first reaction is to say how glad I am for him, but then I hear Molly sob into the phone and I remember the terrible implications of her lover's preferment. The risk of scandal has become so dangerous that sex will have to be off the menu. I am on the edge of the Chiltern Hills and Molly is in Rome. I can't suggest talking the whole thing over at dinner in Trastevere.

'I'm terribly sorry. What can I do?'

Molly wails, 'Give me Penny!'

Penny has already picked up the phone in the kitchen and I hear the beginning of her consolation as she asks gently, 'How long is he going to be in this grand new job?'

The answer emerges as a cry of despair. 'Seven years!'

'Never mind,' Penny is reassuring as always, 'it'll go like a flash!'

I put down the telephone gently, hoping that Penny has brought some message of hope.

Later, when I am in Italy again and at a party after a screening, I talk to an Italian politician, skilled and knowledgeable in the ways of the Church of Rome. I ask him if there is a recognized position in the hierarchy at which sexual activity becomes completely impossible.

'Let me tell you about an old friend. When he was Cardinal of——, he had a live-in boyfriend. He came home one day and said to him, "I'm sorry, I've been made Pope. Our relationship is off. But I'll always remember you and to honour your name I'll take it for my Papal name." And he did.' The old man looks at me, smiling. I don't know if I want this story to be true or not.

*   *   *

> He sipped at a weak hock and seltzer
> And gazed at the London skies
> Through the Nottingham lace of the
>   curtains—
> Or was it his bees winged eyes . . .

Betjeman, Browning, e e cummings, Auden and Lord Rochester—their poetry seems to have been written to be read aloud and is most relished when we go on tour, two actresses, two musicians and I. I am trying to alleviate the withdrawal symptoms since I stopped performing to audiences of twelve honest citizens down the Old Bailey.

There is a drug more potent and producing more ecstatic highs and devastating lows than popping Es, shooting up heroin or sniffing a line of cocaine. This particular narcotic killed Dickens and polished off Dylan Thomas. It drove the old-time barristers to drink and chorus girls, and reduced politicians, who over-indulged in it, to incomprehensible windbags. David Hare has written about the mixed excitement and terror a writer feels when he takes it into his head to perform. He did it in the West End and in the Lincoln Center, New York. I have played the Dumfries and Galloway Festival, several schools (in one our stage was a converted billiard table), as well as more snazzy venues such as the theatre in the Sydney Opera House, the Bristol Old Vic, the Blackpool Grand and a theatre in Brussels. We tell stories and read bits of poetry and snatches of plays. The process of intoxication proceeds as follows.

We stand in the wings waiting for 'Clarence', which is what we pros call 'Clearance', the message from the front of house to the pale young assistant stage manager, dressed in solemn black T-shirt and jeans, often pierced in various quarters of his or her body, who works tirelessly for a derisory wage out of devotion to the theatre. One actress with a stage presence of great purity announces that she is going to fart and retires behind a piece of scenery, a French window or a pantomime cloth to do so. Her muted thunder only increases our panic. The black-clad figure in the corner gives us some cheerful message, like, 'Don't worry if they don't laugh. They never laugh in Watford.' Then I hobble on, supported by an actress and a stick, and sink heavily into a suitable chair, borrowed from a neighbouring hotel or council chamber. We are in a room with one wall missing, a black space out of which we have to produce laughter, even in Watford, or—and this is more difficult—the silence of an audience which is no longer unwrapping sweets and has decided to postpone, at least for the next ten minutes, terminal bronchitis.

At the interval the worst is over. We are chattering inanely. The actress describes being taken from behind while repairing her make-up before the last half of *The Importance of Being Ernest*. But the full effect of the drug, the irresistible high, doesn't kick in until the performance is completely over and I'm in the car drinking champagne out of a warm bottle and eating garage sandwiches. The sense of relief is like nothing else in the world and must be the reason why so many otherwise sane people devote their lives to a profession in which rejection, humiliation and long periods of unemployment are an essential part of life.

The school in our village became empty and Penny wanted the building to be used for holidays for inner-city children. There was some opposition to this plan, mainly from new arrivals in the village who didn't want to see an inner-city child ever again. So a Trust was formed to buy the building and we started performing to help pay back the bank loan. In what seems a disappointingly short time it has been paid off. The prospects are grim. No more arts centres and occasional provincial theatres. No more discreetly farting actresses and scandalous intervals. Above all, no more highs on prolonged drives home, listening to the late-night shipping forecast. I'm facing a prolonged period of detox and rehab, in solitary confinement at home, occasionally telling my stories to the bathroom mirror and getting no reward of laughter.

My addiction is too deep-seated. Before going on to the hard stuff I had been hooked on the softer drug of the law courts. There, the high moment comes not during the drive home, but when you sit down at the end of your final speech. There are no more decisions to be made. Decisions are now for other people. The judge will do his best, speaking as one ordinary, decent citizen to other ordinary, decent citizens, to steer the jury to his way of thinking. They will retire and stay out as long as possible (in long obscenity cases, their ambition was to stay out so long that they had to be lodged in an airport hotel where, so the ushers alleged, they visited each other secretly during the night). They will come back with a verdict which may be unwelcome but is probably reasonable. But, at the high moment when you sit down with your part played out, it is no longer any business of yours.

With such a long history of addiction it is

obvious that I will never kick the habit. I have given in and accepted engagements in Eastleigh Arts Centre, a country house near Malvern, a school in Folkestone and a Georgian theatre in Yorkshire. Since I have stopped being a barrister I have found, on the whole, a more satisfactory way of performing. If we put on a poor show at the Eastleigh Arts Centre, no one's going to prison for fourteen years.

*   *   *

We are doing one of our smartest gigs at the Red Pear Theatre, a converted cinema in Antibes. The place is run by the enthusiastic wife of a retired Far Eastern businessman. We stay in their house and will be playing to large audiences of the English who have decided to retire to the Cote d'Azur instead of Surrey. One of the actresses today is Angharad Rhees, small, blonde and so attractive that the pianist, arriving for the rehearsal, alleges that his hands will be too cold to play unless he can warm them between Angharad's thighs. This problem solved, we start to rehearse and Angharad reads out the first line of John Betjeman's poem about the arrest of Oscar Wilde in the Cadogan Hotel:

'He sipped at a weak hock and seltzer . . .'

This is greeted with uncontrollable laughter from the young English stage staff. When asked to explain, it seems they thought Angharad said, 'He sipped at a weak *cock* and seltzer . . .' Although this might, in some circumstances, have been appropriate for Wilde, it is not what John Betjeman wrote. The effect of this on Angharad, of course, is that she becomes terrified of the line and is convinced that she is going to say 'cock' during the performance. I little know, however, the lengths she will go to in order to avoid this pitfall. She says:

'He sipped at a weak port and seltzer . . .'

Only fear could have produced, for Oscar Wilde, such a revolting drink.

*   *   *

Five lots of children come to the school this summer. One group consists of Russian refugees. I sit in the garden talking to their helpers while the children jump into the pool. The scene is Chekhovian; there are three women looking tired and beautiful, and a couple of gently sorrowful men. Some of them have been in the country for eight years, during which time the Home Office has been unable to make up its mind to allow them a permanent stay. The consequence is that they

43

have no passports, can't go for holidays abroad and, not being allowed to work, can only do voluntary jobs. We talk about changes in Moscow, why Gorky Street has lost its name and the fact that weapons seem to be freely on sale in the kiosks. More alarming stories emerge. A family who wanted to open a ski resort in Russia were threatened with death by a powerful politician. These threats were real enough to drive one of the ladies sipping tea under the tulip tree to flee to England. I say I wish that my daughter Emily could have been with us, because she is fluent in Russian and first fell in love with a Moscow poet named Denis. Sadly she's now in Hollywood being murdered in the cult horror movie *Scream Three*.

As soon as they hear the words *Scream Three*, the children come rushing from the pool, deeply impressed and calling for photographs of Emily. Chekhov, Gorky Street and Kalashnikovs in kiosks have been forgotten in the excitement of hearing of someone who knows the stars of *Friends* and is in a cult American horror movie.

CHAPTER FIVE

I'm at home in Turville Heath. Jessie, who is eight years old, arrives. She is dressed in a

T-shirt and shorts and a cap of the shape once worn by the French Foreign Legion, that is to say it has a flap to save the neck and the back of the head from sunstroke (it's a windy April day). She holds a pen and has come to ask me the questions on the form she has in her other hand. Her job, set by her school teacher, is to discover what amenities those of us who are over sixty possessed when we were her age.

When I was eight years old had we a refrigerator? No. We had an ice-box for which the fishmonger brought large chunks of ice which melted slowly. A television set? Of course not. A car? Yes, a large, hearse-like Morris Oxford. And then comes a question I can't answer at first. 'Where did your Mum go shopping?'

I try to remember. In fact, the butcher, the baker, the grocer and the fishmonger called, not only on us but on everyone in the village, and left boxes of provisions at kitchen doors. Kate Simmons, a pink-cheeked, indomitable woman, walked round with a wooden yoke on her shoulders from which dangled two great pails of slopping, creamy milk which she would ladle out into our jugs.

What else did we have? Bedrooms where the numbing cold was temporarily held at bay by stone hot-water bottles on which you stubbed your toes; a silver tea-kettle boiled by a lamp full of methylated spirit; many ponds, now dried up, but one then apparently clean enough to provide water for making tea; slopping chamber pots to be emptied in the morning; rabbit for dinner, now only served in smart restaurants; two schools within a couples of miles, now we have none; two pubs and a shop in Turville, which now has one pub and no shop. In our nearest settlement the pub (in my childhood presided over by Mabel Hooker, who also, strangely enough, owned a bar in the Place Pigalle) is now going to be sold off, for probably something near half a million pounds, as a desirable residence. We also had an indigenous population of woodmen, chair-leg turners and farm labourers, three pairs of entertaining lesbians and a lady of the manor who had a grey crew cut and voluminous shorts and was given, by her husband the general, an axe for Christmas. She chopped down trees on the common and prosecuted those brave enough to trap rabbits there. Within less than a mile from our door there was a church and a non-conformist chapel, both now turned into expensive houses.

It's hard now to remember how the First World War dominated our imagination. The masters at my prep school were still affected by shell shock and battle fatigue. Some had shrapnel still lodged in their bodies, which accounted for their irrational rages and subsequent spells of equally irrational remorse. In the art class we drew men in tin hats, exploding howitzers and limping khaki-clad figures with bloodstained bandages. Visiting clerics preached sermons about visions of angels on the Somme and urged us to go 'over the top' to our common-entrance exams. We had barely recovered from one World War before we were threatened by another. The wireless, which my father kept beside his place at dinner, to be switched on as soon as he got bored with our conversation, began to report Hitler's speeches. As we were often told that subalterns sent to France between 1914 and 1918 had only a one-in-four chance of survival, my prospects of reaching old age seemed increasingly remote.

None of this has a place on Jessie's form. I return to the question of the shopping and write, 'It got delivered.' Now we are, as Tony Blair would say, 'modernized'. I suppose every age is modern at the time; when I was a child the 1930s were modern, but according to our present Prime Minister the word means 'computer literate'. The wonderful result of the astonishing advance in technology is that you can place your order on the Internet and the groceries will be brought to your door. Time has done a gigantic, mechanical whirligig and we have got back the privileges which we enjoyed in 1931.

*   *   *

The damage to the countryside goes deeper

than the loss of pubs, schools and churches, harmful as that is to rural communities. Near us, down a bumpy road, through the beech trees, in a secret and silent valley, we have a farmer who keeps sheep and cattle. He has a wife and four young children, a radio but no television. His accounts show that after the deduction of his necessary expenses, he is left with a profit of £9 a week to keep himself and his family. He gets income support, and if he talks about the crisis in the countryside, Tony Blair apparently feels justified in asking, 'What crisis?'

After years of neglect and the mishandling of the BSE scare by the last government, the farmers and country dwellers were bursting to vote Labour. Their present mood can be judged by the huge, well-behaved countryside marches and the reception given to bland government ministers pointing out, with singular ineptitude, various alternatives to farming.

Our local sheep farmer should, they say, start a riding school, but he's no horseman and has no money to buy horses. He should open a theme park, but neither he nor the Government have much of a talent for theme parks. He should take in bed and breakfast visitors, but his family occupy all the bedrooms. These solutions can only remind you of the one-legged actor in Peter Cook's sketch who has it in mind to play Tarzan.

The truth of the matter is that the Government is standing back and allowing farming to die, just as Mrs Thatcher presided over the death throes of heavy industry. Twenty-two thousand farmers went out of business last year, and another twenty-two thousand the year before. There's £360 million waiting in Brussels to compensate farmers for the strong pound, but the Government won't take it because they would have to provide matching money—only half the sum blown on the transient Dome. Farmers, some hundreds of whom have been driven to suicide, now have to watch hundreds of millions being handed out to a 'millennium experience' utterly remote from the England of Cumbrian hillsides and Devon villages.

If England is thought of with affection it's often because of our countryside. Our literature, from Chaucer to Shakespeare, Milton, Wordsworth, Emily Brontë and D. H. Lawrence, is seasoned in the country, the fields and the woodlands. It's the business of government to see that it's preserved for the pleasure and sanity of all of us. The fatal mistake has been to imagine that the interests of the countryside are in some way different from the interests of farmers. The countryside can only be maintained by a healthy agriculture. If farming dies, a most precious part of England dies with it.

We're told, on the basis of doubtful and

49

speculative statistics, that 3.8 million new houses are needed to cover our green and pleasant land, 900,000 in South-East England. Such houses, if needed, should be used to reclaim inner cities. We might have suggested they should be used to give jobs and provide benefits in the neglected north, if we did not have it on Tony Blair's good authority that the North–South divide is as imaginary as the crisis in the countryside.

I made some of these complaints to a newspaper and also mentioned the fact that all the cottages which contained woodmen or farm workers in my childhood were now bought, for the odd half a million, by merchant bankers or couples in television. Alastair Campbell, the perhaps over-sensitive New Labour spin doctor, told a mutual friend that he supposed I thought the Government should intervene if anyone caught a cold in the countryside. I am also out of favour with all the local couples who work in television. It's time to go to Italy.

*   *   *

Old age entails a good deal of sitting and staring into space. This is by no means an uncreative occupation. Thoughts, memories, bits of poetry, awful old puns, quotations from bottles of sauce and school hymns float through your mind, and then it becomes a comfortable blank and the body is motivated by no more than a deep reluctance to move. In England old people stare into space in private; they sit at home, or in the sheltered accommodation into which they have been thoughtfully put by the relatives who don't know what else to do with them. In Italy, where we have come for the summer, old men are taken to the café. A chair is set for them, usually at the point where the tables meet the traffic so they are half in and half out of the way. They sit with their hands folded over their sticks, only occasionally exchanging greetings or complaints, doing absolutely nothing until it is time for them to be taken home, fed a little and put to bed.

The old men are set out and are left until late at night in the Cisterna Square of San Gimignano, the hilltop city where families competed to build the highest towers and the cathedral murals luridly depict the horrors of Hell. Now weeds and small bushes grow in the stonework at the tops of the towers and windows look out over a huge, misty plain. In the cloisters the Angel Gabriel, painted by Ghirlandaio, brings good news to Mary as she sits by her bookshelf and her hourglass. The old men are motionless and untroubled. Although this is the afternoon, the touring opera company has arrived and the lights are being hung over the stage opposite the cathedral steps. The square will be packed with a crowd as enthusiastic as any at a

51

football match for tonight's *Trovatore*.

The Kinnocks are here, taking a holiday from their jobs in Europe and are, as usual, cheerful, laughing, generous and, also as usual, have quarrelled all the way on their long drive from Brussels. Neil is Vice-President of the European Commission but still has an underlying sadness, an unnecessary feeling of guilt perhaps, at having lost an election he had prepared the Labour Party to win. Glenys is more fulfilled than she ever has been, as an MEP liaising with African countries. The Kinnocks know San Gimignano well, having stayed there, or with us, on countless holidays, and they are well in with the Communist mayor, the power base of the City of Towers.

Italian Communists, who are slightly to the right of English Liberals, have done well in Tuscany. Siena, if it had been modernized in today's England, might well have been wrecked by shopping precincts, chain stores and supermarkets. It remains a place of medieval beauty which is alive, energetic, humming with activity and, because of the social life of the parishes culminating in the irreplaceable Palio, surprisingly free of juvenile crime. San Gimignano's beauty is also unspoiled. The Communist mayor, friend to the Kinnocks, wears Armani suits, has a beautiful and elegant wife, purrs around in an excellent car and can be relied on for a row of seats at the opera and drinks in the interval.

This year the news is bad. The Kinnocks' friend has retired and a new and younger mayor, a schoolmaster, now represents the Communist Party. We are introduced to him at the house of other friends of the Kinnocks. He has arrived late, driving his own Fiat. His shoes and trousers have quite clearly never seen the inside of Fattoria Armani. We chat him up politely and a police escort is provided, as befits the Vice-President of the European Commission. There are, however, no reserved seats and some of us have to be content with the cathedral steps, and there are absolutely no drinks in the interval. We are left regretting the sad decline of Communism in the government of Chiantishire.

The production itself isn't as good as it was in the days of the old mayor, with principals in medieval costumes and the chorus, improbably, in dinner jackets. Driving out of San Gimignano, almost everyone gets lost in the one-way systems of Poggibonsi, and the Vice-President is no exception. Once we have found the right road the driving of Neil, ex-Transport Minister of Europe, evokes criticism from his wife in the back seat. He finds this irritating. 'Keep quiet, Glenys. Either do the driving yourself or stop talking about it.'

After this the obedient Glenys doesn't say a word. She only whistles, and what she whistles is, 'Whenever I feel afraid, I whistle a happy tune.'

San Gimignano also stars in Franco's film. When Mussolini betrays the English ladies, after Italy enters the war, they are deported from the Florence they love and interned in the City of Towers, where their story ends. The good news is that Dames Maggie Smith and Judi Dench are to play the leading *Scorpione*. In the high summer the air is loud with grasshoppers, lizards dart across the hot paving stones, the landscape is blurred with heat and Franco arrives with his driver and secretary to do more work on the script and to make the best of the new stars.

Samantha, the secretary, is sharply pretty, wears glasses and has her father's *Carabinieri* badge on a chain round her neck. Franco is taking photographs and I ask the driver, 'What will you do when Franco and I are working on the script?'

'Watch television.'

'I'm afraid we haven't got a television set. Why don't you go up to the pool? You may find at least five topless women . . .' At this point I offer the driver a pair of swimming shorts, which he angrily throws back at me. 'That would be a disgusting sight!' He is outraged. 'I would never wish to see a woman topless!' When he has stalked off in a dignified fashion, Samantha tells me that the driver would have very much liked to have visited the pool. 'He is,' she tells us, 'a closet heterosexual, a fact which he is anxious to keep secret.'

We do some work and have a long lunch on the terrace. We drink a good many bottles of Chianti from the local castle, which is young, light and leaves no trace of a hangover. Franco is at his best with stories of his great mentor, Visconti, and Maria Callas, whom he loved. After another bottle of the Cacchiano wine, he speaks at length about the pyramids of Egypt. These great mausoleums, he says, were not built by human beings but suddenly appeared in all their glory in the desert by some supernatural force which we don't fully understand. This is one of Franco's dearly held beliefs, such as the wickedness of abortion and the genius of Puccini. It's hot in the afternoon sun, we refill our glasses and we are perfectly prepared to believe him.

*   *   *

Now I'm sitting among the old men in the Bar Dante, the centre of life in Radda-in-Chianti. Huge lorries thunder by to take the hairpin road to Castellina and Poggibonsi. Girls come roaring up on red motorbikes, young men shout at them, Germans fix up automatic cameras to take photographs of themselves, and the old men, unemployed and unoccupied, sit on the plastic chairs waiting for death and smiling in their sleep. Strangely enough, I'd rather be here than in any other bar in the world.

How long ago was it that I was having dinner with my family in an open-air Radda restaurant when we were approached by an incensed English mother and father, accompanied by a pretty, undeniably pregnant, blonde daughter? 'Look at this girl! It's entirely your fault!' the mother said in front of my friends and family. I protested that I had never met their daughter and was certainly not responsible for her condition. 'Yes you are,' the mother was relentless. 'You should never have written that book making Tuscany sound so irresistible!'

In fact I had just written *Summer's Lease*, a novel concerned with the lives and habits of the English in Chiantishire. Now the daughter is married to Fabrizio, owner of the Bar Dante, and today is their daughter Francesca's birthday; it's not so long since that encounter in the vineyard restaurant. Over a coffee and cognac at breakfast in the Bar Dante I congratulate the fair-haired child for whom my book was once blamed.

*   *   *

I first met Muriel Spark long ago in Arezzo, the town of Petrarch and Vasari and the great frescoes of Piero della Francesca. I was with Emily, then a teenager, and Muriel told her, I think rightly, that work should be confined to the old and the middle aged; the young should sleep a good deal, rest and look as beautiful as possible.

Now we are driving across the hills eastwards to visit Muriel and her friend, Penelope Jardine. They live in a converted church where the priest used to tempt local girls with plums from his orchard.

We are in what were once the priest's quarters, where there was found, buried under the floor, bones of what the villagers described as 'dead Christians'.

Muriel, bright eyed and pretty faced at eighty-one, speaks in a slow, amused, Edinburgh accent, full of irony. She remembers the difficult time she had with Marie Stopes, the early and fearless advocate of birth control, when she was working for the Poetry Society and editing *The Poetry Review*. Marie Stopes had been living with Lord Alfred Douglas, Oscar Wilde's 'fatal lover'. 'An arrangement,' Muriel said, 'which would satisfy any woman's craving for birth control.' Muriel introduced poems with irregular rhythms and strange ideas to the readers of *The Poetry Review* and Marie Stopes led a campaign against her choices, disliking Muriel because 'I was young and pretty and she had succumbed to the law of gravity without doing anything about it.' Her criticism became so tiresome and bitchy that Muriel wished devoutly that Marie Stopes' mother had been keener on birth control.

Although a Catholic convert, Muriel no longer goes to church because the priest at Monte Oliveto preached a sermon instructing his congregation to avoid contraceptives. She took exception to this, not out of respect for the memory of Marie Stopes, but because she thought that at her age it was unnecessary to raise the subject. She has now come to the conclusion that preaching sermons is a mortal sin.

She has a great interest in crime, and when she was young and alone in London she lodged in the house of Christmas Humphries, an unusual barrister who managed to combine being the senior prosecutor, in the days of the death penalty, with a conversion to Buddhism. His father, Mr Justice Humphries, was a small, meticulous, hanging judge who started his legal career as a very junior counsel in the trial of Oscar Wilde. Muriel tells us a story about the elder Humphries which I find strangely haunting.

John George Haigh was convicted of the Acid Bath Murders. He lived in a Kensington Hotel, where he was known as a 'charmer' by the elderly lady residents. Having charmed them he invited them to visit his 'factory', which was, in fact, nothing but a store room at

Crawley in Sussex. There he shot them, and dissolved their bodies in sulphuric acid stored in a forty-gallon drum. Detected by the discovery of a surviving denture proved to have been used by a Mrs Olive Durand-Duncan, one of his victims, Haigh was tried at Lewes Assizes in 1949 before Mr justice Humphries and, despite his plea of insanity, sentenced to death.

It is Muriel who provides the chilling epilogue to this story. The years went by, the judge's wife died, and he felt he was rattling around in his large London house. Then he remembered the Haigh case and the name of what seemed to him to be a rather agreeable hotel in Kensington, where it was only too easy to make friends with elderly ladies. Accordingly, he moved into the hotel where the 'charmer' Haigh had also been a guest, and stayed there until he died. Muriel takes great delight in this story, and I am grateful to her for it.

She was treated with wonderful generosity by the two great Catholic novelists. When he was reviewing her first novel, *The Comforters*, Evelyn Waugh was writing *The Ordeal of Gilbert Penfold*. Both books deal with the hallucinatory effect of taking too many pills for sleeping or slimming, and Waugh wrote that he thought Muriel's book was better than his. Graham Greene, who also admired her writing greatly, paid her a small monthly income on condition she promised never to pray for him.

At the height of her success she left England for Rome, where she thought she might receive less attention and lead a quieter life. She advertised for someone to help her sort out her books; so Penelope, then studying art, came into her life. Tonight Penelope also has stories to tell. She remembers the remote descendant of the seventeenth-century poet who wrote 'Go, lovely rose—tell her that wastes her time and me.' This woman, when asked to back up a little in order to allow another car past, said, 'My name is Lady Waller and I do not reverse.' She also has a sensational family story. It seems that her father was, during the war, in command of a section of the British Army stationed in West Africa. He got a message from the commandant of a German force stationed in another African state that promised him merciful treatment after the war if he handed his forces over to the Reich. Having received this offer, Penelope's father wrote to the Foreign Office saying that he had devised a master plan for winning the war. He would ask to discuss the deal with Hitler, secure in the knowledge that the German Chancellor had not had yellow fever, from which Sir Douglas Jardine had recovered. Therefore he'd go to the meeting with a box of Swan Vesta matches packed with yellow-fever germs. During the conversation he would fill up his pipe, produce the matchbox and release the germs. Hitler would catch yellow fever and die, and so the German war machine would collapse.

The answer he got from the Foreign Office was a curt dismissal. It was the silliest plan they had ever heard of, they said, and furthermore, to kill Hitler in that way 'wouldn't be cricket'.

CHAPTER SIX

We are in urgent need of three million pounds. The Lottery grant of twenty-one million towards the twenty-eight million needed for rebuilding the Royal Court Theatre came with a sting in its tail. You might think that if the masters of the Lottery thought a theatre was worth rebuilding they would pay for it all, but the 'matching money' has bedevilled all the theatres that have been chosen to benefit, and the quest for it has ruined at least one provincial playhouse. In the Royal Court's case, we have to find it or face disaster. The search for the missing seven million pounds dramatizes the conflict between the received morality of the theatrical left and the harsh reality of life in the arts today, when political ideals can lead to nothing more satisfactory than a large hole in the ground on one side of Sloane Square.

The hole-in-the-ground prospect is not one that alarms the old guard at the Court. An unfilled hole will show up, surely, they say, the inconsistency of the Lottery and the callousness of the Arts Council, and will cause such a public outcry that the Government will be shamed into writing us a cheque. This argument ignores the fact that governments, of any colour, are no longer capable of being shamed into anything, and bailing out arts facilities in trouble is not high among the preferences of the focus groups which now rule our country.

From various businesses sympathetic to the arts, companies and corporations, all of which are being badgered by theatres with similar problems, we manage to raise a surprising four million. The remaining three are a nightmare, an apparently insoluble problem. It has become clear that if we fail, the Arts Council is not going to bail us out. The hole in Sloane Square, apparently welcome to some, now gapes wider.

And then, descending like a rescuing god on a piece of stage machinery, comes Alan Grieve, a soft-voiced, grey-haired solicitor and Chairman of the Jerwood Foundation. Mr Jerwood, it seems, made his considerable fortune in pearls and is now dead. The Foundation is anxious to distribute part of its capital; it has already put on plays by young writers at the Court, and has founded the

62

Jerwood Library in Cambridge and a large rehearsal and exhibition centre south of Blackfriars Bridge. When I meet Alan Grieve, he presents me with a bottle of Chianti from the castle of Brolio, near where we stay in Italy, and says he would rather like to give us three million, provided Jerwood is acknowledged in the title of the theatre. The Jerwood pearl fishers have long since put back into harbour and, unlike the Tate or the Sainsbury Wing of the National Gallery, the title won't be advertising sugar or groceries.

This life-saving proposition, brought with a gift of wine to an office off Fitzroy Square, causes a horrified reaction among the old guard at the Court which spreads to the young writers, who hold protest meetings denouncing any deal with the Jerwood Foundation as a craven sell-out but failing to indicate any alternative source of the missing three million. This is although one or two of the writers who are so shocked might have been able to contribute a sizeable chunk of money to save the fair name of the Court.

It can be assumed that anyone parting with three million wants something for their money: but how much exactly? There are suggestions that theatre might become the Jerwood Royal Court. But is there, hidden somewhere in the protocols of history, some ritual ban against putting a word before 'Royal' in a title? We would rather like this to be so, and I undertake to research the subject.

'Sorry I can't give you a final answer.' Everyone's away on holiday. Buckingham Palace is almost completely empty.' I have telephoned the Lord Chamberlain, in charge of the Queen's household, and he is doing his best. 'Actually, it's a bit of a grey area. But I'll put you through to someone who might know the answer.'

I am put through to Colonel Somebody who hasn't gone on holiday. He is in the Palace and starts by telling me what I already know. 'It's a bit of a grey area, actually. I mean, you certainly couldn't call it the Tesco's Royal Challenge Cup or the Sutton Seeds Royal Rose. But,' he adds usefully, 'the use of the word "Royal" depends on the Home Office. I suggest you ring up Mavis Longbridge there. She should be able to tell you the whole story.'

'No. Mavis isn't here. She's on holiday and we really don't know when she'll be coming back. I'm Jenny Simpson and I may be able to help you. What's your problem?'

I tell Jenny the whole story and thankfully she is prepared to help. 'I'll do my best to explain it to you. Ring me back when I've finished my sandwich.'

I allow time for the most careful chewing of the most generous double-decker and get Jenny back on the line. 'Quite right,' she says. 'It all depends on the advice the Home Secretary gives the Queen. You'd better write him a letter.'

So the name 'Royal Court', no doubt plucked from the air, perhaps by the man who invented small revolving stages for his naked show girls, is to come under the close inspection of the Sovereign and a high officer of state.

'I don't know if you could hurry it all up a bit,' I suggest to Jenny. 'It's rather urgent. You see, I'm desperate for three million pounds.'

'So am I!' Jenny, full of sandwich, is laughing happily.

I control myself when I'm writing to Jack Straw. I keep off the subject of abolishing jury trials or displacing the burden of proof or forbidding cross-examination in rape cases or the outrageous suggestion of cancelling *habeas corpus* and confining the mentally sick without trial. I merely ask him to consider the tricky matter of the use of the word 'Royal' on a small Sloane Square theatre, and hope Her Majesty will shine a clear light on this notably grey area and satisfy the writers by giving 'Royal' priority over 'Jerwood'.

Without much delay, Jack Straw writes that Her Majesty wouldn't tolerate any word going before 'Royal'. Alan Grieve is prepared to agree to the two theatres inside the Royal Court building being called 'The Jerwood Downstairs' and 'The Jerwood Upstairs'.

*   *   *

Constructing the new Royal Court proves to be a long and difficult business. With buildings on each side and nowhere to park lorries, the operation, like keyhole surgery, has to be carried out from the top, reaching down to the excavation under the square. Digging out the restaurant, between the Tube line and a sewer, is a delicate undertaking. While this is going on, painfully slowly, we move into two West End theatres, the small Ambassadors and the large Duke of York's in St Martin's Lane.

Stephen has knocked these theatres into shape. He makes another theatre in the round out of the dress circle of the Ambassadors, with a small acting space and the audience on the stage below it. He has roughed up the foyer of the Duke of York's so it gives the sort of gritty welcome appropriate to a theatre of passionate protest. For his first production, a play about Northern Ireland called *The Rat in the Skull*, the stalls are covered over with clanging iron prison corridors on which the action takes place.

Stephen announces that he is bored. He is prepared to stay with us until the building is finished, but he doesn't want to choose the plays. He doesn't really want to direct them. He wants, it seems, to make a film, the secret ambition of all British theatre directors. The spirit that led him to the Italian circus, to put on a red nose and have buckets of water flung in his face, has come on him again and he wants to be off. Less sympathetic voices suggest it was the same spirit that led him to construct an elaborate house on the stage for *An Inspector Calls* and then destroy it at the end of the last act.

So Stephen remains the supremo of the building, and after long talks with a number of contenders we appoint Ian Rickson as the new Artistic Director. He's had great successes directing *Mojo* and *The Weir*, a magical play by Conor McPherson which keeps our whole enterprise alive during an extraordinarily long run in the Duke of York's. Ian goes to a number of writers' meetings, at which he listens sympathetically to complaints that the sacred name of the Royal Court is being shamefully sold off for a measly three million. As the protests grow louder, Timberlake calls for my immediate resignation, a request I am strongly tempted to agree to. Alan Grieve telephones and says he was invited to a meeting in Peg's Place, a small club somewhere behind Shaftesbury Avenue.

'Do you know who Peg was?' he asks me in dread, and adds, 'I imagine she was some kind of prostitute.'

*   *   *

Show-business history contains many famous and dramatic scenes. Up till now my favourite has always been the great encounter in Manchester Gaol when Sam Spiegel wrestled for the soul of Robert Bolt. Bolt was writing *Lawrence of Arabia* at the time, but, having refused to be bound over for sitting down in Trafalgar Square as part of a CND demonstration, was sent to gaol, so work on the script was rudely interrupted. Sam Spiegel's Rolls Royce drew up at the prison gates one misty morning and in the ensuing scene, equal only to the Emperor kneeling to the Pope at Canosa, the great producer begged the writer to forget his principles and return to work. What was said exactly, we now, with both parties dead, have to invent. It's enough to know that the scene ended with Bolt being transported in the Rolls Royce out of confinement and back to the Connaught Hotel.

This was the stuff of drama, but now it has a rival as Alan Grieve describes his experiences in Peg's Place. This is, in fact, an entirely respectable club, but he gave the impression that after he rang Peg's bell, an eyehole opened and he was subjected to a hostile scrutiny before being admitted to some scene of drunken debauchery. He was then, as I imagined it, led past writhing bodies until he was admitted to a smoke-filled back room in which a daunting trio awaited him.

There was, as Alan describes him, a cross-looking man with heavy glasses and a black sweater, whom I take to be Harold Pinter. He also speaks of a daunting woman, a slightly exaggerated description of Caryl Churchill, and a 'smooth-looking man' who turns out to be David Hare. 'They lectured me for an hour,' Alan says. 'Then I told them I couldn't agree with a word they'd said and I left Peg's Place.' Never, I imagine, to return.

Timberlake still thinks, despite all assurances, that taking money from businesses and the Jerwood Foundation would risk the independence of writers. She gives an interview to the *Guardian* in which she says she is the only writer on the Board, although Nicholas Wright, a distinguished playwright, has been on it since Max's days, and I have also written plays. As the details of the agreement with Jerwood are being finalized, she resigns.

Stephen and Ian have been to more protest meetings, no doubt with the intention of calming the writers' nerves. Alan Grieve wants them both to sign a letter of support for the agreement. When Ian shows a momentary hesitation I find myself moved to make as passionate a speech as Timberlake had been by the cause of thrush. Stephen, I say, dreamed up this new building and now, instead of getting it finished, he, Ian and some of the writers were massaging their tenuous senses of morality. I don't go so far as the director of another subsidized theatre, who

69

said that all writers wanted was to have their plays put on, even if the funding comes from General Pinochet; but I say that I feel the writer's job is to write and it is our responsibility to see that he or she gets a theatre. At the end of this somewhat corny oration, Stephen says it's the most exciting meeting he's ever been to and gives me a kiss.

CHAPTER SEVEN

The Duke of Wellington and Lord Uxbridge are standing together on the Field of Waterloo. A bouncing cannon-ball knocks off Lord Uxbridge's leg. After a long pause, Wellington says, 'My God, Uxbridge. You've lost your leg!' At which Uxbridge, looking down, agrees, 'My God, so I have.' True or not, this story represents the kind of stoicism with which we'd all like to be able to approach disaster, illness and eventually death. My father's blindness was something he did his best to ignore. I never even said, 'My God, Dad, you can't see', as Wellington might have done. And I suppose his refusal to make concessions to his disability was stoical.

I'm discovering more about the Stoics: the fact, for instance, that Seneca was tutor to the young Nero, surely the most dangerous job in the history of the teaching profession. It must have strained to its limits the Stoic belief that we have little choice but to go along the road, however rough, that Fate has chosen for us and try not to complain. Another old Stoic said that we have as much free will as a dog tied to the tail of a cart. He can run a little from side to side, and bark loudly, but if he tries to stand still his lead will strangle him. He has no power over the driver of the cart.

It is also a popular misconception that free choice brings wisdom, tolerance and reliability in old age. Some of the worst misdeeds, crimes and follies of mankind are committed by irresponsible old men. The experience of old age is that, in a body maimed and incapacitated by time, you feel much as you did when you were eleven. The great weight of years, the unexpected experiences, the happy and terrifying moments are still judged by eyes fully opened in the playground. If, as Hemingway wrote, the seeds of what we do are in all of us, you easily spot, in that same playground, the little judges, the embryonic criminals, the future revolutionaries who will sell their souls to the establishment, the good eggs and the smarmy hypocrites, the poets and the critics, the teachers and the taught. In the dormouse summer, it seems to me, we have very few choices left to us; most of what we flatter ourselves by calling great decisions merely consist of following paths already mapped out. It was probably easy for St Paul's school

71

friends to judge that here was a child who would be subject to a remarkable conversion on the road to somewhere or other.

Such beliefs provide difficulties for priests and lawyers.

The idea of sin requires some degree of choice between right and wrong, and free will is as essential to the workings of the Old Bailey as wigs, gowns and the stairs down to the cells. Prison sentences depend on the belief that criminals and judges exercise some sort of freedom in their choice of profession, and yet the Central Criminal Court is, by and large, a place where the children of judges and lawyers are sentencing the offspring of muggers, fraudsters or receivers of stolen property. The stern words of condemnation and the unconvincing protests of innocence are spoken by those whom, it can only be fairly said, the cart has pulled in different directions.

These are the thoughts in the back of my mind when I'm caught up in the affairs of the Howard League for Penal Reform. I've agreed to be the host of a money-raising lunch in Wormwood Scrubs prison. The great and the good, or the not-so-great and somewhat-less-good of a generous disposition, are going to pay £200 each for a meal with the prisoners. The money is to be devoted to the League's researches into alternatives to prison. All governments, mainly concerned with votes at the next election, shut their ears to claims that prison is often a cause of crime and not a solution to it. At least, government ministers are fond of saying, people don't commit crimes when they're in prison, ignoring the fact that prisons are the scenes of drug dealing, grievous bodily harm and frequent homosexual rapes. We imprison a higher percentage of our citizens than any other country in Europe, which either means that we are more criminally minded than other nations or that we have an unthinking faith in prison. As 20 per cent of prisoners reoffend, such faith would probably be ill founded. It's to investigate such ideas, and inform arguments, that the Howard League, named after the prison reformer John Howard, exists. We used to call it the Penal League for Howard Reform because of the Conservative Home Secretary Michael Howard's blind faith in prison as a cure for evil, gaol for children and the abolition of the Right to Silence. We now have a Labour Home Secretary, Jack Straw, who follows all too faithfully in his predecessor's footsteps, only his name is harder to turn into a joke.

Now the canteen in Wormwood Scrubs sees chat-show hosts, merchant bankers, members of the House of Lords and a few writers sitting at small tables with prisoners, sharing grey mince, lumpy mashed potato and digestive biscuits, washed down by tepid water from a light-blue plastic mug, and having a friendly

73

chat.

Penny and I sit with a puzzled young man who lost his job as a house painter in the North. Hearing in a local pub that £1,000 was being offered to anyone prepared to travel to Africa and return with illegal substances, he decided to take up the offer. Naturally, being a complete amateur, he was caught and naturally, in the confused state of the prison service, he is locked up far from his wife and the child he hasn't seen for two years, who believes he is away on a painting job. Expecting a visit from her, he has stained his fingers with prison paint to make his story more probable.

Over our heads there is a net, presumably to protect the ground-floor prisoners against suicides and falling objects, and above that the gallery from which the more serious convicts look down on us like an audience in the upper circle. When the lunch is over, I rise to thank the prisoners for entertaining us and explain that it isn't my fault that any of them are inside because I haven't practised as a barrister for over ten years. When I say this a voice pipes down from high above our heads. 'The lifers are upstairs, John!'

As we come away from Wormwood Scrubs the Chairman of W. H. Smith comes up to complain. 'I've never had a worse time,' he says. 'I pay £200 for a disgusting lunch and the prisoner I sit with turns out to be a major shareholder in my company. He did nothing but cross-examine me about the annual general report!'

*   *   *

One day when I was working in Pinewood Studios, wearing my ignoble script writer's uniform, I was queueing as usual for my canteen lunch when I noticed a nun in front of me piling her tray with all the Woolton pie and carrot cake available. She turned to me and was wearing, I noticed, with her nun's habit, lipstick. 'I think it's being a virgin,' she said, 'that makes me so bloody hungry.' I got the message. She wasn't a real nun, she was an extra in the film *Black Narcissus*. We had left the dull world of documentaries for the endless possibilities of fiction. Peace had broken out, I left the Crown film unit and wrote my first novel.

In the shallows of another millennium, a dozen novels later, of course the habits and passing obsessions of the world have changed. Perhaps the common culture you could once assume in the reader, a working knowledge of Shakespeare, the poems in the *Oxford Book of Verse* and the history of England, the reliable store of knowledge which Evelyn Waugh and P. G. Wodehouse, for instance, could use for their jokes and which formed the basis for crossword clues, has now been fragmented. No

75

one learns poetry at school, Wordsworth and Browning are no longer taught and history begins with the origins of the 1914 war; who remembers the Repeal of the Corn Laws or the Battle of Waterloo? This apart, the tasks of the novelist, telling a story which lures the reader into turning the page, creating characters and evoking aspects of the passing scene, remain the same. At least this is what I am telling myself, with ebbing confidence, as I start off on another American book tour.

New York means the Public Library, the Barnes and Noble bookstore near the Lincoln Center and the Wyndham Hotel. You can get a large suite at the Wyndham for less than the price of a cupboard-like single in a London hotel. There's no room service and your breakfast comes up in a brown paper bag from the deli across the street. There are kind, elderly porters to bring you up in the lift and a friendly reception from Mr and Mrs Mados who own the place, which is generously extended to English actors, writers and directors. If you grow tired of the contents of the brown paper bag you can cross the road for breakfast at the Plaza Hotel. That small area between West 58th Street and the Park has long been the hub of my existence in New York. It is there that I meet the ingenious conman.

I am walking from the Wyndham, past the entrance to the Plaza, bound for the cinema round the corner, when a charming, youthful and handsome black man greets me with a glad cry.

'Amazing!' he says. 'Fancy seeing you in New York! And you're looking so well!'

Limping with a stick, having an afternoon off in the middle of a book tour, it seems improbable. 'Am I really?'

'Blooming. So amazing we should run into each other like this!'

'I suppose it is rather . . .' I am playing for time, waiting for a clue as to who the hell this young stranger who is so glad to see me might possibly be.

'Still, you know what I mean. It's a small world.'

'I suppose you could call it that.'

'A very small world, when you and I just bump into each other in New York!'

'Quite a coincidence.' I am still playing for time.

'You wait until our friend in England hears how we just happened to bump into each other!'

'Our friend?' I prick up my ears, thinking I'm going to get a clue.

'Yes. Our great friend! Our black friend. He'll be tickled to death when he hears we met in New York. Just by chance. And you looking so cheerful and blooming.'

'Which friend,' I am feeling my way carefully, 'is that, exactly?'

'You know. Our *black* friend.'

I look blank and the mood changes. He gives me a look of sad accusation. 'You don't mean to tell me,' he says, 'that you haven't got any black friends?'

Immediately I feel guilty. I've got black friends, haven't I? But do I have enough black friends? What does he mean exactly? Not Tabitha. Not Elsie. Who, then? For some reason I think of a black actor, Tom Mabele, who I've worked with recently. 'Oh. You mean Tom Mabele?'

'Of course! Who else?' A smile of delighted recognition spreads across his face. 'Old Tom's going to be over the moon when he hears we bumped into each other in New York!'

Will Tom really be over the moon, I wonder? But then the young man I might know is off on another enthusiastic tack. 'We can't just leave it here,' he says, 'we've got to celebrate. Have an evening. You free for dinner?'

'I'm terribly sorry. I'm talking at the Public Library.'

'Too bad. Tomorrow night, maybe. We got to get together!'

'I'm going back to England tomorrow.'

'Where're you staying?'

'The Wyndham Hotel. It's just round the corner.'

'OK. What do you say I call for you in the morning, drive you to the airport?'

'It's quite all right. I've got a car ordered.'

'I'd just love to drive you. Give us a real chance to talk and get up to date about old Tom. Know what I mean? Look.' He makes a grand gesture towards the traffic and Central Park. 'My car's parked over there. Room for all your luggage.'

And, as I look for a parked car among the passing yellow taxis and carriages with their sad, bony horses, he comes to the point at last. 'Only trouble is, I'm right out of gas. I'm on my way to buy some from the gas station, but I need twenty dollars deposit on the can. Just till tomorrow morning . . .'

I am filled with admiration. It is such a sparkling performance, with the master stroke of making me feel guilty about the number of my black friends, that I decide to give him twenty dollars for his time and I start to count them out. When I get to ten and pause, he looks hurt and angry.

'I said *twenty* dollars.'

'Oh, fuck off!' I lose patience and, instead of protesting, or grabbing the rest of my money, he looks hurt and slinks away. I feel unaccountably guilty.

*   *   *

I have one other experience of a mugging. This is again in the vicinity of the Plaza Hotel. I am crossing the road from the Plaza Oyster

Bar to the Wyndham at around ten o'clock at night when a large figure looms up at me, dressed in a dark overcoat buttoned to the chin and a black leather cap.

'Give me fifty dollars!' The voice seems to come from some deep, nether region and to float up like steam from the subways.

Suddenly I become a young barrister again, determined to settle the case on the best possible terms for my client who is, at this particular moment, myself. 'What would you say,' I smile hopefully, 'to twenty-five?'

'All right,' the voice rumbles up, it still seems, from beneath the street. 'Give me twenty-five dollars.'

He takes the money and melts into the shadows beside the deli, and I go to bed in my hotel room. I seem to have met a very reasonable mugger.

*   *   *

Book tours all over the world, from Sydney to San Francisco, are very much the same. The talks in public libraries, the rush to sign everything possible ('A book signed is a book sold,' my first publicist told me), the evenings with a long-suffering publicity girl, all too used to authors who tell them that their wives don't understand them and make unattractive advances. 'I'm not any good at sex,' one British author had admitted to my travelling companion. 'But with you, Sue, I'll really *try.*'

American book tours are usually enjoyable, and I feel I have reached some sort of fame here, because Rumpole was mentioned during the O. J. Simpson trial, which the nation watched on television a year or so ago. One of the defence lawyers got up and said to Judge Ito, 'Your Honour, I think that, as Mr Rumpole would say, we're getting a case of premature adjudication.' This is, in fact, something that Rumpole does say. I am also on my way to visit the Rumpole Society in San Francisco, where the Rumpolians meet in a reproduction of Pommeroy's Wine Bar and stage 'She Who Must Be Obeyed' look-alike competitions. I am very proud of my effect on San Francisco. Years ago, I adapted Evelyn Waugh's *Brideshead Revisited* for television. Although Waugh, when he wrote it, didn't think that more than eight Americans would ever like *Brideshead*, the series enjoyed a considerable success in America and led to Lord Sebastian look-alike contests, also in San Francisco, with many young men carrying teddy bears down to the Marina.

Before I left England, I had met Robert Halmi, who produces lavish films of well-known stories for Hallmark Television. I had enjoyed writing a version of *Don Quixote* for Halmi, he had already done *Ulysses* and now wanted me to have a go at 'Jason and the Argonauts'.

I liked the idea of writing about the Greek gods, who seem to me, more than the gods of other civilizations, to be excellent characters for comedy. In New York I meet an understanding and helpful woman from Halmi's office who brings me the strange and wonderful account of Jason's voyage by Apollonius of Rhodes. The representative of the Network, however, is not so helpful. She says she 'spun the story to her boss by presenting Jason as a simple hero'. She is also fairly cool towards the idea of light-comedy gods, engaged in bitching about each other and constant sexual infidelity. I'm afraid that I might be setting out on a journey as fraught with difficulties as that of the Argonauts.

*   *   *

Boston is perhaps the American city most accessible to the English. It's the home of Harvard and Lochovers, a proper restaurant with a great nude painting over the bar, sympathetic Irish waiters and excellent fish, including the strangely named scrod. Lochovers joke: a visitor at Boston airport said to his taxi driver, 'Do you know where I can get scrod?' Taxi driver: 'That's the first time I heard that word used in the pluperfect subjunctive.'

I'm shown into a bedroom in the Boston Hotel, which, no doubt owing to some carelessness on the part of the computer, hasn't been cleaned since its last, apparently energetic, occupation. The ashtrays are loaded with cigarette ends, the sheets on the unmade bed are stained and there are dirty Bloody Mary glasses under it. The bathroom towels, strewn about the place, bear traces of blood. I grab the telephone and ask the desk clerk to send someone up to clean the room and get the Manager to ring me at once. I am an English visitor filled with righteous indignation.

Two minutes later, the telephone rings, and a small voice says, 'Mr Mortimer. Sir.' 'Forget all the sirs!' I am in an explosive mood. 'This room's a tip! It's the most disgusting mess I've ever seen. Let me tell you, sir, there are stains on the bed sheets. There are Bloody Mary glasses under the bed. There's blood on the towels and the ashtrays are overflowing with . . .'

'I'm really sorry about your troubles.' The voice is polite and soothing. 'But I'm the Manager of the Smithsonian Institute in Washington. Just ringing up about your talk . . .'

At the end of the tour we drive to Madison across huge wheat fields, north of Chicago. Now and again the great, empty landscape is punctuated by an isolated shopping mall, surrounded by cars. Madison is in a cheese-producing area and its inhabitants, at times of

83

celebration, wear hats shaped like huge cheeses. My hotel window looks out on an apparently boundless frozen lake and I see people cycling across the grey ice. Then small keel-less sailing boats skitter across, and holes are made in the ice for fishing. Brave people speed across it in four-wheel drives. In March, I am told, the lake starts to thaw. The first four-wheel drive falls in and occasionally its passengers drown. Then the inhabitants of Madison know that spring has come at last.

CHAPTER EIGHT

When the announcement is made telling you that the happy years when you could put on your socks are over, it's natural to wonder which god, if any, has pronounced this sentence. This is because it won't be very long before you will find out for certain.

My recent experiences with the Greek gods have made it clear that these deities are quite unsuitable for family viewing on American television. Dealing with Jason, not a particularly exciting character, who might be described as the Bulldog Drummond of Greek mythology, a dim-witted hero to whom terrible things keep happening, I discover that he was tremendously fancied by Hera, Zeus's wife and the Queen of the gods. In fact, she went to the lengths of turning herself into an old woman, so that Jason might carry her across a stream. Deceitful, promiscuous and constantly jealous of each other, the gods are more interesting, and more human, than the hero. Zeus has the habit of turning himself into various animals for the purpose of surprising and having sex with mortal women. Such behaviour was not to be mentioned on the Network.

Not to be mentioned either was Jason's wife, a far more interesting character. Her knowledge of magic and spells was of considerable use to her husband; she even went to the lengths of cutting her younger brother into small pieces and dropping him in the sea to delay their pursuit by her furious father. She dealt with Jason's mistress by sending her a dress which burst into flames the moment she put it on, a plot well in line with the behaviour of the wife in *Fatal Attraction*. Dealing with Medea, whose name is derived from the Greek word for a deceiver, we were instructed by the Network to present her as an innocent and impressionable girl, a mythological reincarnation of the younger Doris Day.

Having failed to strike the correct note on Olympus, my next job for Mr Halmi concerns the God of Israel. Dickie Attenborough is producing some stories from the Old Testament for Hallmark and I choose King David. This should be safe enough, I think, because surely there will be none of the weaknesses of the vain and promiscuous Greek gods recorded in the Bible.

Reading through Samuel and the Book of Kings, however, you find remarkable similarities to the behaviour on Mount Olympus. God the Father has Zeus's partiality for burnt sacrifices. He delights in the smell of smouldering heifers and becomes dangerously wrathful if they're not regularly provided.

It's also worth remembering that the God of so many kindly and human worshippers had a distinct taste for ethnic cleansing. The reason He turned against Saul was because that King, chosen by the prophet Samuel, had spared the life of King Agag and saved the best sheep and cattle of his people, the Amalekites, although God had instructed him to 'slay both man and woman, and infant and suckling, ox and sheep, camel and ass'.

The story I've been writing is of David, the shepherd boy, who played the harp to soothe Saul's nerves and ended as the shivering old King whose son revolted against him. David's racist utterances remind you of a bad day in the Metropolitan Police. When attacking Jerusalem he said, in the words of the 'Good News Bible', 'Does anyone hate the Jebusites as much as I do? Enough to kill them?' No doubt David had many faults, and putting his mistress's husband in the forefront of the battle was almost in the Medea tradition of ruthless behaviour. But he had a wonderful moment of chivalry when he could have killed the sleeping Saul (now his enemy), but only cut off a piece of his cloak to prove how close the old King had come to death. When he dances in front of the Ark wearing nothing but a loincloth, and goes home to the wife who tells him he's made a fine fool of himself in public, we know exactly how he felt. However badly he behaved, God couldn't help loving David.

I heard that John Braine, the author of *Room at the Top*, used to talk about God's favourites, who are allowed a certain licence. 'God looks down on London,' Braine said, 'and sees this one and that one committing fornication and adultery and he says, "It's no good, you know. That's not allowed. You're going straight down to hell." And then he looks down on Hampstead and sees—' (here he named a well-known woman writer and social star), 'and sees her betraying her husband and fornicating away and he says, "You know, I rather like you. So carry on." Well, that's what he said to King David. "I rather like you."'

*   *   *

After this encounter with various religious beliefs, I remember that C. M. Bowra wrote, 'A people gets the gods it deserves. The grinning, gloating ogress of the Aztecs mirrored a race brutalized by incessant war.' So the Greek gods are as louche, and often as charming, as their worshippers. The God of Israel is extremely nationalistic and frequently cross. The Scotch God is prim and meticulous and the American God, at any rate on the Networks, wishes to be taken literally, lacks a sense of irony and prefers large financial contributions to burnt offerings. When I was at school I was introduced, in the Chapel, to the Church of England God, a well-intentioned old gent who doesn't care too much for religion.

'Having closed our eyes to the eternal substance of things and opened them only to the shower and shams of things,' wrote Carlyle, 'we quietly believe this Universe to be intrinsically a great, unintelligible perhaps.' The state of mind of believers and unbelievers alike is now to look on God as the Great Perhaps. A. N. Wilson's book *God's Funeral* deals with the nineteenth century's increasing scepticism; men and women had to bury a deity they had come to regard as man's invention and, in spite of themselves, shed tears at the funeral. My father was a convinced Darwinian, who told me, early in my life, that it would have been impossible to create a horse in six days, or even six centuries.

Darwin's discoveries made it obvious that the world was far older than the six thousand years attributed to God's creation, and that species evolved over long periods of time instead of being instantly produced. The controversy over evolution produced a delightful character, Philip Gosse, father of Edward who put him into a book. Gosse the elder was a zoologist and Plymouth Brother who thought of an original way to reconcile Darwin and the Bible. Why shouldn't the Great Perhaps have made the world in one grand gesture, but filled the Garden of Eden with fossils and other interesting but purely decorative proofs of old age? Gosse the younger said his father's ingenious theory only caused atheists and Christians to look, laugh and throw it away.

But Philip Gosse's God, scattering misleading clues, seems an amiable practical joker, and Gosse a kindly man anxious to end a quarrel.

*   *   *

Franco's film is now in production. He called me and I found myself back in Rome. The money was in place, the completion guarantee was signed. The casting was settled and, Franco having found a boy attractive enough to play himself, the starting date had been fixed. I agreed to return to the house of the shades in Cinecitta with David Sweetman, an English writer who had helped Franco with his autobiography and who was going to correlate our various versions of the script.

So I sat in one room, writing dialogue with a lukewarm electric radiator pressed to my thigh. My pages were then carried to another room where Franco, upright on a high chair and still in severe pain after his hip operation, was persuaded by David Sweetman not to change too much.

We had the most trouble with a scene in which the young Fascists break up Doney's tearoom. David and I knew the English ladies would only say some line like 'Terribly bad manners!' or 'Very odd. There's glass in the sugar.' But Franco wanted them to behave like Violetta at the approach of death.

So now the film is in production. The great Dames and Lady Olivier simply learned their lines and spoke them, which is all you can hope for. In Hollywood, some actors seem to say whatever comes into their heads, with the result that the dialogue is only dimly reminiscent of a writer's work. Some performers also have difficulty separating the character they play from themselves. 'I couldn't say that,' an actress once told her director. 'It's anti-feminist.' 'It's not you that's saying it,' he was at pains to explain to her. 'It's the character in the film that says it. Don't worry—it's called acting.' If this attitude to drama spreads, there'll be no one left to play Iago or Lady Macbeth.

It must be some lingering effect of the method school that causes actors not only to want to play parts, but be them. An English director working in Hollywood said an actor there referred to Hamlet as '*my* character', as though Shakespeare had no part in its creation. He also told me that he was shooting a night scene in a garage forecourt which called for complicated lighting and intricate crowd movements. After three hours of preparation, the star of the show emerged from his Winnebago, glanced round the brilliantly lit forecourt and said, without a moment's hesitation, 'My character just wouldn't park here!'

It's very hot this summer, and like a furnace in the garage in Rome which has become the schoolroom in which the *Scorpione* are imprisoned. In one lunchbreak, the Dames and the Lady went to Franco's house, one of them told me, and as he wasn't due there for lunch, stripped off all their clothes and leaped into his pool. Franco reappeared unexpectedly with a young man who played one of the *Carabinieri*. At the sight of the great pillars of the English theatre completely naked, they leapt back into the car and beat a hasty retreat.

*   *   *

Prospective customers for the 'Soxon'

machine, those who move around airports in wheelchairs or bleeping buggies, people seen tottering towards aeroplane lavatories unaccompanied by lovers and supported on a stick, need escorts, preferably friendly, to accompany them on journeys.

Back in England I am due to visit Edinburgh for a television festival, and my wife is coming with me to provide entertainment, moral support and to scout out the wheelchairs. Understandably, she decides to forgo this treat and visit Emily, in Hollywood. I have to look for a friendly guide.

On a nippy evening at an outdoor opera, I had met a singularly beautiful girl named Tabitha. I told her I was writing a script about King David, and with no sort of ulterior motive I happened to mention the fact that when he was stricken by old age, King David got extremely cold in bed, however many blankets were piled on top of him. Faced with this problem, his courtiers found a young Shunarnmite girl named Abishag, who consented to lie on the King to keep him warm in the night.

Faced with a lonely journey to Edinburgh, I ring Tabitha and invite her on a trip to Scotland, dinner in the Café Royal and Oyster Bar, a night in the Balmoral Hotel and, perhaps less tempting, a debate on the future of television. To my delight, she accepts the proposition, only adding that she intends changing her name to 'Tabishag'. The only worry is that the unchangeable ticket was in my wife's name, a part that Tabishag would have to play, if only on the shuttle.

We are met at Edinburgh airport by a woman from the Festival, who greets us warmly and tells us, in the car, that Richard Eyre is staying in our hotel and will give, that evening, the James MacTaggart Memorial Lecture to the fortunate delegates. This is the best possible news to me as Richard Eyre, who ran the National Theatre with such unerring success and twice staged unforgettable productions of *Guys and Dolls*, is one of my best friends, as is his wife, Sue Birtwhistle, who produced the television version of *Pride and Prejudice*. 'Is his wife here too?' I ask our hostess. 'Oh yes, I think so,' she assures me. I look forward to a memorable dinner with them at the Oyster Bar.

Arrived in the Balmoral Hotel, I stand at Reception and ask for Richard Eyre's room number. They say 308 and I write him a hasty note. 'I'm tired of my wife,' I tell him, 'who's always off on trips. So I have got a new wife, a staggeringly beautiful black girl named Tabishag. What do you say we all have dinner together and celebrate?' I give the note to the porter and ask to be put through to Room 308. There follows a rather strange conversation with a secretary.

Me: Is Richard there?

Secretary: Yes. But he's rather busy at the moment.

Me: What's he doing?

Secretary: Rehearsing the James MacTaggart Memorial Lecture.

Me: I've done that. Tell him not to rehearse. It's much better if you do it off the top of your head. Put him on, will you?

(PAUSE)

Secretary: What did you say your name was?

Me: John Mortimer.

(PAUSE)

Secretary: Did you say Clem Mortimer?

Me: (at an increased volume): *John* Mortimer.

Secretary: I don't know if he's got time to speak to you.

Me: I'm sure he has. Please. Will you just tell him I'm here and I do want to speak to him.

A long pause follows and then a still, small and completely strange voice comes on the line.

Strange Voice: Richard Eyre speaking . . .

It is only then that I remember that there are two Richard Eyres in the world. One ran the National Theatre and the other is not only high up in the world of television, but is a born-again Christian. And my letter about ditching my wife in favour of a beautiful Tabishag is winging its way to the wrong Richard.

It takes some nifty work by the hotel staff to recover the letter before it is delivered. But perhaps, when it comes to elderly television writers, they travel most safely who travel alone.

CHAPTER NINE

I arrive home from a theatre in London. I go to sleep in the car and awake to hear the dogs barking as they dance as near as possible to the wheels and pretend to get run over. I come in to my writing room, taking off my tie, yawning, longing for bed and notice that the little red light on the answering machine (now known as Voice Mail) is flashing. This produces the usual feeling of faint gratitude, a comfortable sense of not having been entirely forgotten, but wanted by somebody. I push the button and a hoarse and urgent voice greets me. 'Animal Murderer John Mortimer, QC. We know where you live and we're coming to get you.'

I sit down, amazed and, in some sense, flattered. Someone's offering to kill me—why on earth should they bother?

*   *   *

'I shouldn't open that one, John. I'd just drop it straight in the bin.'

The speaker is Terry Bucket, who delivers our letters. He was also elected, by a huge majority, to the local council and became, in due course, Mayor of Henley.

At his inauguration party we saw Terry in his chain of office, his lace and velvet, and were filled with pride. His daughter, Donna Bucket, who has been voted Miss Henley, is the author of some surprisingly erotic verse which her proud father brought to show me. Today, what he is bringing has nothing to do with adolescent love. It is a rule of the Post Office that Terry has to deliver all parcels, regardless of their content. Even so, Terry and I both realize he is delivering shit.

Death threats and crap through the post are, it seems, the inevitable result of taking part in the argument about fox-hunting.

*　　*　　*

I have never hunted. Once, when I was about fifteen, I did shoot a rat with an air gun, but I have never since caused the death of a single animal. I was brought up in the country, where hunting seemed a natural and reasonable way of controlling foxes. Hunting forms a great part of our literature. Siegfried Sassoon, disgusted by the killing of human beings in war, wrote memorably about it. Anthony Trollope, most humane and understanding of storytellers, hunted regularly, although, being short-sighted and overweight, he tumbled into hedges and ditches almost every time he went out. Such people were not sadistic blood-thirsty fiends who took a pleasure in killing. Penny has just been hunting in Ireland. When she asked one of the regulars how often they caught a fox, he had to admit, 'Not within living memory.'

So far as I'm concerned, anyone's at perfect liberty to detest fox-hunting, to think it's absurd and awful, wish to have nothing to do with it and seek to persuade hunters to give it up. What is ridiculous is to turn it into a criminal offence and drag manacled masters of fox hounds and pony-club girls into our overcrowded prisons. We live in a time when one section of society longs to enforce its particular habits and preferences on others,

97

who may enjoy a completely different way of life. I detest karaoke and morris dancing and the views of the Shadow Home Secretary, Ann Widdecombe. But I wouldn't have any of these, even Ann Widdecombe, made a criminal offence.

I am watching a hunt meet in front of a country house. The hounds collect in a white wave of wagging tails. Warm wine and cold sausages are handed out. The foot followers assemble—grey-haired couples in tweed hats, sporting parsons with walking sticks. Then the motorized saboteurs arrive in elderly vans with their packed lunches, some in flak jackets, some disguised in IRA-style balaclavas.

They are prepared for war with the riders, hurling abuse or stubbing out cigarettes on children's ponies. The hunt moves off, battle is joined and an enjoyable day's sport, in the course of which many foxes will escape unharmed, will be had by all. As usual, life in the English countryside is red in tooth and claw.

It's an odd comment on our times that fox-hunting has become the one issue to be regarded by a confused public as a matter of life and death. The euro and proportional representation are met with nationwide yawns. War over Kosovo awoke no ancient patriotism, and Northern Ireland has simply gone on too long; but more than 400 Labour MPs packed the chamber to discuss an anti-hunting bill.

The next week, when a measure concerning disadvantaged children was debated, the place was almost empty.

The Earl of Onslow, in a pronouncement which is almost a sufficient justification for the retention of hereditary peers, said, 'In my youth, the Church of England was anti-buggery and pro-fox-hunting. Now, strangely enough, it's pro-buggery and anti-fox-hunting.' The present excitement about hunting is due to the decline of religion. G. K. Chesterton said that when people stop believing in something, they don't believe in nothing. The reverence once accorded to the ancient gods is now given to animals, to whom all human virtues are attributed, regardless of the fact that foxes have absolutely no concern for animal rights and England's favourite pet, the cat, murders millions of small birds and mammals for fun, drawing out the killing process with sadistic glee. Recently, a three-legged deer was given an artificial limb and put back into the woods, where it no doubt met an early death, and in Sweden, a man caught spanking his wife with a live eel was fined heavily for cruelty to the eel.

*   *   *

The countryside march is a remarkably cheerful and well-organized counter-protest. More than a quarter of a million people proceed from the

99

Embankment to Hyde Park and, unlike many smaller political demonstrations, it's without violence and, happily, with jokes—'Eat English Lamb—Most Foxes Do' is on many of the placards and the afternoon is mercifully unpolitical. I walk for a very short time beside Lord Tebbit, the archetypal Thatcherite, who is, on such an occasion, an unexpectedly charming companion. Penny, momentarily tired of carrying a sign which reads 'Labour and the Countryside United', asks Tebbit to hold it for a while. In the belief that the message is 'Labour and the Countryside Untied', he carries it cheerfully for quite a long way before he realizes his mistake.

I have almost forgotten the hoarse-voiced animal caller, who knows where I live. Penny, warned by the police to be careful of parcels from unknown sources, finds a razor blade concealed in an envelope and survives with all her fingers. I forget to look under the car for bombs, or behind bushes for shadowy figures in the dark garden. Many people, after all, live with death threats and I've only had one. I find myself sitting at dinner opposite Tom King, former Secretary of State for Northern Ireland and naturally the recipient of many death threats.

'Don't worry,' he is laughing, 'if they mean to kill you they don't ring up and talk about it. They just do it anyway.' I don't know whether I find this particularly reassuring.

Now I am talking to a party of Royal Court supporters, making a speech in which I touch on current events such as death threats and peculiar parcels through the post, before homing in to important matters such as Government funding for the Arts. When I finish, someone calls for questions and, after the usual embarrassed silence, a grey-haired, pearl-necklaced woman near me wants further and better particulars.

'What *kind* of shit was it?' she asks.

*　　　*　　　*

'He really is getting old, isn't he; why do you stay with John? Is it love or duty?

The question was asked by Philip Gould, Master of Polls, organizer of focus groups, whose big toe is always testing the water of public opinion before New Labour plunges in. I hadn't met Mr Gould at this point, and nor had Penny until she found herself sitting next to him at dinner. So his question was by way of an introduction to a new acquaintance.

It's not a bad point, however. What was it that made my mother stay with my blind, irascible, unreasonable and, in many ways, impossible father? Was it love or duty that made her dress him, cut up his food, lead him round the Law Courts and sit in the train reading the embarrassing evidence in sensational divorce cases aloud to him? Was

101

she really sufficiently interested in gardening to lead him round and describe the slow progress of every shrub and hardy perennial? Did she find it easy to guide his fingers as he pricked out seedlings, or weeded the ground about flowers he could never see? What were the rewards for her devotion? A husband who would laugh until the tears ran down his face when he was in a good mood; but who was capable of shouting at all his helpers if his egg was soft, or his bath cold, and would ask the God he didn't believe in if he were 'totally surrounded by cretins?'

Why did my mother put up with it? She was no down-trodden, subjugated Victorian woman, bound as a slave to a tyrannical and demanding father of the family. She had been an Art student who read Bernard Shaw's *The Intelligent Woman's Guide to Socialism and Capitalism.* She had shipped herself out to South Africa before the 1914 war, ridden bareback across the Veldt and swum naked in Natal streams. She would greet any mention of the Royal Family or of most politicians with incredulous laughter. She had no religious faith to force her to sacrifice her freedom, and perhaps her happiness, for the sake of constant attendance to the needs of a blind husband. Nor did she know what she was getting. My mother married a Second Lieutenant in the Inns of Court Volunteer Rifles who, although short-sighted, was likely to be sent off to ritual slaughter in France quite early in their married life. Just as Penny married a midle-aged QC still capable of shinning up a few hundred steps in Positano and standing on his hind legs for anything up to six hours in the Central Criminal Court for the purpose of making a speech. Penny is a strong-minded woman, as was my mother, capable of giving physically fit lovers the boot without compunction or regret.

So why do they do it? Does love really survive bad temper and failing joints? Is it a point of honour to stand by our friends and relations? Is staying on to put on other people's socks the mark of a truly heroic character? I would say, undoubtedly, yes.

Of course, my mother did have her temptations. I can remember times when she would steal away in the middle of dressing my father and leave him with his braces dangling, yelling out 'Kath! Kath!' in increasing panic. She would go down to the kitchen, make herself a cup of tea and wait till he had learned not to class her among the cretins.

When I was young, taking my father on one of our walks across damp fields, over stiles and through woodland paths, I often felt tempted to escape the loose-skinned hand on my sleeve and run off to a secret hiding place in the bracken. So my father would be left, I thought, blundering and shouting in the darkness; but I never left him so.

I'm sure Penny is similarly tempted, waiting for me to go down a short staircase as carefully as if I were descending Mont Blanc. In picture galleries, at parties, out shopping, she will dart away, only to return miraculously later. But why? Unable to think of an answer to Philip Gould's question about love or duty, she said, I'm sure doubtfully, 'Probably both.' Later our friend Elizabeth suggested, as a *réponse d'escalier*, an answer only thought of on the way out, 'It's because of the wonderful sex. But I don't suppose you'd know about that.'

*　　　*　　　*

At least half of today's post consists of begging letters, soliciting for various charities. Children are exploited in such letters; there are heart-breaking photographs of them maimed or starving, with swollen stomachs and covered with flies. We receive such letters without anger and shell out when we feel like it. A good deal of my time is spent in begging for money for the Royal Court Theatre or the Howard League or to cure river blindness. Begging is, in many parts of the world, an honoured profession and, for members of religious orders, a necessary source of income. Politicians beg for votes, advertisers beg for sales and many stars of television beg shamelessly for attention. And yet when gypsy mothers, shunned in their native countries,

104

appear begging in Underground stations, the public recoils in horror as though stretching out your hand for a few coins were a mortal sin.

I have to say that I still hold to these views notwithstanding the events that occur when *Tea with Mussolini* is opened to the public.

Franco comes to England for the film's opening in the Empire, Leicester Square. He has undergone another operation and we meet at a South-East Asian restaurant, part-owned by David Sweetman, opposite the Maida Vale tube station. It's a Saturday night, the food is excellent and the restaurant crowded. Asking if we'd care to see the results of his operation, Franco stands up, pulls down his trousers and shows off a long, neat scar which stretches, it seems, along the sturdy white flesh of his hip to his knee. The Thai diners around us are watching fascinated until the Maestro pulls his trousers up and gets on with the green curry.

The film does fairly well in England and much better in America. We go to the Italian première in Florence, which starts with a reception in the Palazzo Vecchio. In the Great Hall of the Five Hundred, decorated by Vasari, Franco sits above us on a sort of throne, the long scar now covered by smart suiting. The Mayor makes a speech praising him as the spirit of Florence, and Franco responds graciously.

The film is dubbed into Italian, so the jokes calculated to show the snobbishness, the

105

insularity or the pretentiousness of the English expatriate ladies lose their point and we don't get a single laugh. However, at the end many of the audience seem moved, some are in tears and they all rise to applaud Franco.

Next day, the town is as beautiful as ever, the Arno full and placid and the streets already clogged with tourists. Making slow progress towards the Medici tombs, I am confronted by a woman carrying a baby, which couldn't have been more than eighteen months old, wrapped in a blanket. She holds out her hand, into which I put a probably too small amount of money. She thanks me by touching me, then covering my chest with the blanket. Safe from view in this tent, the child aims unerringly for my inside pocket and pulls out my wallet. I call for Penny's help and retrieve my money from the baby's tiny clutches. Then I go on, thinking of a Europe in which the towns are surrounded by displaced people, asylum seekers, victims of ethnic cleansing or other nationalistic cruelties, with no other means of support than training their children to pick pockets as the pre-nursery-school part of their basic education.

So my association with *Tea with Mussolini* and our visit to Florence end appropriately, with the director enthroned in the Palazzo Vecchio and the writer being mugged by a baby.

CHAPTER TEN

I am walking along a narrow pathway by a stream, in a garden where roses, geraniums and hibiscus are flowering in January. High in the trees a woodpecker is monotonously at work. Beside me walks Rashid, a slim figure in a long white gown, white backless slippers and a small cap. We move as though we were a bridal couple parading up the aisle; we tell each other bad jokes in appalling French and from time to time join in singing the Marseillaise. He helps me to a table under an acacia tree, wet with dew in the early morning. The day will be as hot as a good English summer, but over the tall palm trees we can see the silvery line of snow on top of the Atlas mountains. Rashid will leave me here until lunch-time. This is a daily routine for me in Morocco.

Some time ago I met Jack Profumo. He was walking with a crutch but looked extremely healthy. Profumo, who has spent his life working in Toynbee Hall, in the East End of London, to atone for his part in a forgotten scandal, said he had been in Morocco staying at the Gazelle d'Or Hotel. He told me he had been looked after by a charming young Arab called Rashid, but complained that Rashid had taken him, every morning, to a table under an acacia tree and sat him down at a table where 'he told me I had to write until lunch-time'.

So here I am, writing in black ink on the long pads of lined paper, now hard to come by, such as we used to take down the evidence in Court. I need to fill four pages, twelve hundred words, before lunch. And in no time at all, it seems, the waiters are arriving in their long white gowns, as tactful and concerned as good surgeons. One, middle-aged and apple-cheeked, has as his lover a professor from Saratoga, with whom he spends his annual holiday. The other waiters call him 'L'Americaine'. There is Bled, a tall and beautiful young man, black as some Moroccans are, and Absolon, older, with a bad leg, who bears a remarkable resemblance to Pandit Nehru. I call Booda, the head-waiter, *le Grand Fromage*, or the Big Cheese, an idiotic joke which makes all the white-skirted waiters double up with laughter. The former old head-waiter, who wore heavy horn-rimmed spectacles, walked with a curious loping stride, delivered comic one-liners punctuated by giggles and was known to all the English visitors as Peter Sellers, is no longer here.

We used to fly to Marrakech, with its bustling, aggressive market and its vast square filled with snake charmers, letter writers and dealers in various magic cures and pungent, unlikely medicines. From there, it's a four-hour drive over the Atlas to Taroudannt, the

Gazelle d'Or's nearest town. This journey is not recommended to nervous passengers, as the road soars up above the snow line and hovers on the edge of sheer precipices.

You can hear the wailing horn of a bus a long time before it appears. Then it will squeeze past you on the inside, forcing you uncomfortably close to the edge. About halfway across the mountains, you can stop at a small French bistro with checked tablecloths, vin rouge and steak and pommes frites. The French built the good roads which join all the towns in Morocco; and almost everyone speaks French.

On the road across the Atlas you will come, miles from anywhere, on a boy in a bright djellaba, holding up a piece of quartz, a glittering semi-precious stone, tempting you to stop and bargain; or a man selling oranges at a rickety table. If you stop for a picnic in a completely deserted place, with not a sign of human habitation for miles, as soon as you open your basket, twenty or thirty children will appear from nowhere, all smiling politely, waiting patiently for a sandwich, or a cigarette, or a few dirhams, which they will hold in clenched fists as they scatter away. The same crowd of spectators will gather if you stop to pee.

At last the road comes down from the mountains, named by the Greeks after the unfortunate hero who had to carry the weight of the world on his shoulders, and you see the long, pink, castellated walls of Taroudannt. This is a much smaller, quieter, gender town than Marrakesh, with less aggressive salesmanship in the souk.

You can wander among the great sacks of spices, the dangling lanterns and spread-out carpets. You can buy, if you really have to, the second-hand false teeth displayed in a small shop window. There is a place where you can buy live chameleons, shaped like Lilliputian dinosaurs, in wooden cages, or, if you believe in magic, the dead bats and dried iguanas which, the Berbers say, will bring you perpetual happiness. Twice a week, the country and mountain people come into Taroudannt to sell their sheep and goats in the market. The blue-dressed women from the Sahara, after a long journey by bus, hold out a couple of chickens or a live rabbit for sale at a street corner. Musicians and hucksters rattle up in *petits taxis,* which are cheap and rarely carry less than eight passengers.

Down a side street in Taroudannt is the old head-waiter Peter Sellers' house, every wall decorated by the murals he has painted of Moroccan landscapes, Arab arches, sandy beaches, the sea, and women in bright, biblical clothes with half their faces covered. His paintings have the colours of Matisse and, since his time working in a restaurant in France, he has written poetry. His older, student children ask for English books and long to escape from the Third World into, at least, the Second. His youngest totters across the stone floors and collapses, laughing, on a low couch. The huge television set is never switched off. Peter Sellers gives his visitors presents, wrapped in newspaper; a painting, an antique water bottle, or perhaps a dagger.

No hotel guest now notices his resemblance to the famous film star, because the painter-poet has become too ill to be a waiter.

*   *   *

The working waiters lay the tables, and spread out a buffet lunch. They are remarkably unmoved by the sight of so many salads, such varieties of fish and sizzling kebabs, nor are they moved to envious rage by us eating in the middle of the day, because it is Ramadan and they can neither smoke, eat, or swallow a glass of water until six o'clock this evening. After that they will await, this Friday, with eagerness and hope, the rising of the moon. If it's fully and gloriously visible, they can eat tomorrow. If it's hidden among the clouds, they will have to wait until Sunday. It's now twenty-nine days since they saw the sliver of moon which started Ramadan. Twenty-nine days of daily starvation, and sullen discontent among the airport staff, a minor inconvenience demanded by God and directed by the appearance of the moon.

111

The hotel's Moroccan owner, Rita Bennis, is the granddaughter of a King's Vizier. She was a child in the harem where her grandfather had dinner with each of his wives once a week. There is a story that this grand Vizier had a number of black female slaves whom he taught to play Mozart quartets. Descendants of these musical servants, who are Rita's cousins, can be found working in the garages and shops of Taroudannt. She met her Italian husband, Marco, in a square in Rome, so their marriage is a genuine reconciliation of the Catholic and Muslim faiths. Now Marco runs the farm attached to the hotel, with its many sheep and two cows whose bells can be heard tinkling among the orange trees. He's having a hard time, because the existence of the European Common Market makes it impossible for him to export his thousands of tons of tomatoes and tangerines across the Straits of Gibraltar and into Spain.

A few years ago, I came here with my daughter Emily. Our pleasure in each other's company was hardly affected when the quiet, respectable English visitors, who spent their days round the pool reading John Le Carré and Joanna Trollope, or wrestling with the crossword in back numbers of the *Daily Telegraph*, cut us dead and hurried past us in the restaurant with their breath held and their faces turned, as though we had brought mad cow disease to Morocco.

Fed up with this, we decided on a trip to Essaouira, once Mogador, on the Atlantic coast between Agadir and Casablanca. The town, once Portuguese, has wide, bone-coloured beaches on which we used to see camels led down to have their feet washed, white walls and deep-blue doors and window-frames.

It also has the Villa Maroc, an old house, now a hotel full of antique Moroccan furniture, and two of the world's best fish restaurants, one which looks out over the sand and one on the harbour jetty. Sitting in 'Sam's', you can see the fishing boats, painted as brightly as those on Van Gogh's canvases, bringing back the loads of fresh fish, oysters, lobsters and sea urchins which you will be having for dinner.

When I first came to Morocco, the roofs and chimneys were covered with toppling storks' nests and the big, white, flapping birds rose up above the minarets. Camels were everywhere and pulled ploughs through the red earth. Now the storks have mysteriously vanished and we only saw one camel when we drove to Essaouira. However, we did get an unforgettable Moroccan spectacle. Emily and I had stopped for petrol and suddenly the garage forecourt echoed to the thunder of horses and rifle fire. The place filled with a platoon of galloping Arab cavalry with glittering, chiming harnesses, brightly coloured cloaks and turbans; with one hand delicately fingering a loose rein, each man held up and fired a long, silver-plated gun. Bullets peppered the clouds. This was the 'Fantasia', the ornate charge for the King's birthday celebrations, being rehearsed outside a Total garage.

An important character in the life of the Gazelle d'Or is Adam. You may not, for days at a time, catch sight of him, but when you sit in the big hall of the hotel, in front of a log fire having a before-dinner drink, you'll hear a piano being played with all the skill and flair of those in the great drinking clubs, the White Room and Muriel's, in the forties. The repertoire is eclectic: 'Thanks for the Memory' may melt into Strauss's Four Last Songs, and 'Joshua, Joshua—Sweeter than Lemon Squash You Are', into an aria from *La Traviata*. Adam is tall, with a somewhat exaggerated moustache and appealing eyes. He has a past in the army and some diplomatic connections and Rita heard him playing the piano at a party in Rabat. He takes the breakfast orders, and his chief role is as a friend.

In the way of friendship, I asked him why the English visitors are shunning us.

'It's quite simple,' he says. 'They think you take Petronella Wyatt on holiday.'

Petronella, is the daughter of the late Woodrow Wyatt, a politician, journalist and Thatcher worshipper. She's busy writing columns in the newspapers and is an unlikely travelling companion for me. Emily is not particularly thrilled with this information.

*   *   *

Writing is timeless, bound by no period in the writer's life, free to wander backwards and discover, in the past, a present to remember. Covering pages of the legal pad under the acacia tree, I can be whatever age I choose. And then I look at the backs of my hands. All I can think of is my father's hands, the brownish skin, tanned by hours in the garden, hanging off thin bones. Then I realize that I'm looking at my own hands, the lightly suntanned skin hanging like a loose glove.

As I swim, my father's quotations from Shakespeare wander round my head—the lines he repeated because he enjoyed their sound, as some people hum tunes. When the cook used to bring in his breakfast he often greeted her, in a loud voice, with, 'Nymph, in thy orisons be all my sins remembered,' to which she might reply, 'Here's your bacon.' Other favourite snatches were 'The multitudinous seas incarnadine' and 'Give me your hand. Come you from old Bellario?' a question he regularly asked me. Then I remember a line from *King John* which gave him enormous pleasure. Hubert the gaoler is about to have little Arthur's eyes put out. He gives instructions to the executioners, who are hidden behind the curtain, saying:

> . . . when I strike my foot
> Upon the bosom of the ground, rush forth,
> And bind the boy . . .

'Rush forth and bind the boy,' my father repeated thoughtfully, 'it sounds like a rather dubious firm of solicitors.' After that, whenever he met a lawyer he didn't know well, he used to say 'Are you from Rushforth and Bind-the-Boy's, then?'

I remember him laughing and then I look up and see the white-gowned figure of Rashid standing at the end of the pool, waiting for me with a towel and a walking stick to help fish me out.

*   *   *

The waiters laugh helplessly at the suggestion that the end-of-Ramadan celebrations might include *le whisky*. But their laughter is nervous. Will they see the moon this Friday evening? In their homes, carefully hidden, are presents for their children, new T-shirts and trainers, djellabas and backless slippers. Will they be able to give them out tomorrow, or do the children have to wait for another day in hungry suspense? The ghostly figures are staring at the night sky which might, or might not, be too cloudy to put an end to weeks of starvation. Then there is a stirring, a buzz of excitement and a cry of recognition. There has now appeared, from behind a cloud, the thin sliver of the moon which started their penance. Ramadan is over. They come back into the hotel laughing, with more jokes about *le whisky* with the couscous. It's so easy for gods to give pleasure by imposing a period of fast.

* * *

I can swim in the pool at the Gazelle d'Or with Rashid's help, and emerge unaided from the bath at home, where the wall has hand-holds, which are as welcome as crevices to rock-climbers. There is always a thrill of panic at the end of the bathing process—will you make it to dry land or crash back, humiliated, into soapy water? Throw out a leg and feel for the bath mat, pull upwards and clutch the edge of the bath between the buttocks. A push and a pull on various handles and, magically, you're out, sitting safely, home and prepared to be dried. But when it comes to strange bathrooms, I have learned to play for safety since my near-fatal encounter in Australia, in the years before the disaster with the red-hot pokers.

The Sydney hotel's bathroom had no pretensions to simplicity. It was the sort of facility which would have looked at home in the Roman palace of the late Emperor Nero. Marble covered the floor, marble steps led up to a circular bathtub into which water spouted from the mouths of lions. The touch of a button would produce a whirlpool of Scylla-like proportions. Getting out of it, barefoot and naked, and descending the marble steps, I had a momentary vision of myself as Fred Astaire, my childhood hero, dancing down a long white staircase as a climax to some brilliant routine.

And then I pirouetted down the steps, across the wet floor, to crash into a set of glass shelves which held shower caps, cotton-wool buds, packets of soap, pot pourri and the complimentary fragrances of a generous hotel. I fell amongst splintering glass and a hailstorm of cotton-wool buds, aware of a torrent of destruction and dizzy from the Jacuzzi.

Picking myself up, I retreated to the bedroom and, to soothe my nerves, put Mozart's C Major Piano Concerto on the sound system, also thoughtfully provided. As I sat listening, I glanced at the white carpet and saw my feet on a growing scarlet circle—the crashing fragrances had produced a number of shallow wounds. There followed a desperately amateur effort to remove traces of the crime. Scrubbing with wet flannels and face towels only extended the bloodstains, so the place soon looked like the scene of an axe murder.

When I rang to tell the housekeeper that the place looked like Marat's bathroom after his assassination, she took it calmly and I was offered a room on the ground floor, usually reserved by Helen Montague, a well-known theatrical producer who was away on tour. I moved in and discovered that the bath was at ground level, sunk into the floor. I must have overfilled it and, when I immersed myself, I noticed the bath mat floating away down the passage.

Meanwhile, Helen Montague returned and was told that her room was full, and was offered my previous accommodation. She was too busy telephoning to notice the state of the carpet, until a huge machine with whirring brushes, exuding soapy foam, was pushed in over the floor. 'Just the usual procedure,' they told her, concealing—the room's immediate past. 'We always do it when a new visitor arrives in this particular room.'

My encounter with the ornate Jacuzzi had, apart from anything else, twisted an ankle. I had one of my first wheelchair rides through Sydney airport, where cheerful Australians in shorts waved at me and called out, 'G'day Rumpole!'

119

CHAPTER ELEVEN

I am visiting my first wife, Penelope, who is very ill. She sits, smiling, grey-haired, in a neat flat in North London, looking out on a sunny garden which she has induced to flower profusely. She's with her eldest daughter, Madelon, who was nine when I first met her and is now an elegant grey-haired woman who has left her house and dogs in France to look after her mother. Co-co, a small white poodle, frisks and capers about the room in a way which makes Penelope laugh. Our son, Jeremy, has taken time off from producing radio dramas to be there. Penelope has difficulty breathing, and from time to time fits an air mask across her nostrils. I remember her father, a small, squat rector in a Cotswold village, whose faith in God was slowly petering out. As the years went by, he could believe fewer and fewer of the Thirty-Nine Articles. However, he had to admit that he was unqualified for any job outside the church. In these circumstances, he gave up preaching sermons and substituted a show of films, on vaguely religious subjects, in the church. The primitive projector he used gave him painful electric shocks, and so, during Evensong, he wore a pair of gumboots under his surplice for the purposes of insulation. He was eccentric, irascible, a heavy smoker and I was very fond of him. Unable to leave her much else, he passed on his passion for cigarettes and his terminal lung cancer to his daughter.

It's probably as difficult for two writers as it is for two actors to be married to each other. Penelope and I were grasping for the same events, but longing to write about them as though they were ours alone. She wrote wonderfully, and got great pleasure from describing the awfulness and absurdity of her experiences. She was the only person I have ever known who could find serious fault with the Champs Elysées, but only she could have turned our lives into such good novels. We lived together dramatically, often sliding to the edge of some disastrous precipice. It was, you might say, never dull.

She is the Penelope who, when properly angry, might drive the car into the garage wall and then back up and crash it again, and again. At a lunch with a film producer, she could, after the first course, get up to go to the lavatory and never come back. When she first met Penny, she said, 'If you'd turned out to be an articulate, intelligent, talented woman I'd've been jealous, but now I've met you, I don't mind at all.' She was, and at eighty still is, beautiful, and when I first met her, surrounded by the children of various fathers, we talked endlessly in all the neighbourhood pubs and wrote songs together. But now our marriage has been over for thirty years, during which time Penny and I have never been able to think of a suitable reply to her denial of jealousy.

We discuss the children, those we have in common and those fathered and mothered by others. We spend an hour behaving with the politeness of strangers. Penelope has become a devotee of the stand-up, impromptu comedian Eddie Izzard. She is surrounded by his tapes, videos and signed photographs. She says that when she dies she wants to be remembered as Penelope Mortimer, Writer, Gardener and Eddie Izzard fan.

*   *   *

'Do you mind if we fight the Trojan war in your garden?'

Jeremy is on the phone. Radio plays, with which I started as a dramatist, are hard to write and call for great effort of imagination in the listener. True aficionados say they prefer them to television dramas because the pictures are more satisfying, and there is some truth in that. My son has spent most of his life in radio drama, but a change has taken place and now radio plays are no longer done in studios with actors standing round a microphone pretending to be half their age, with split coconuts clattering as horses' hooves.

Radio has gone out on location, partly in search of the right atmosphere, but also because under the strange and convoluted manner of John Birt's management of the BBC, the Drama Department now has to pay heavily for the use of its own studios. 'Of course,' I tell Jeremy. 'If you think my garden sounds like the plains of windy Troy, do use it.'

So a minibus arrives, containing a distinguished cast of actors, including Maggie Smith's son, Toby Stephens.

'Where do you want to start?' I ask Jeremy.

'In a hermit's cave on Mount Ida—so could we use the potting shed?'

'Of course. I'm sure the potting shed sounds almost exactly like a hermit's cave on Mount Ida.'

Then a spare bedroom upstairs is chosen as the perfect sound-setting for a sex scene with Helen of Troy. The most difficult request comes at the end of the day's work.

'We want to fight the Trojan war on your lawn. Do you happen to have a sword?'

'You're in luck's way,' I tell Jeremy. 'I mean, there must be many houses on the edge of the Chiltern hills without a single sword between them. But I happen to have a sword leaning up against the grandfather clock, with a sheath to go with it.'

It all goes well. Actors draw my sword and bang it against its metal sheath. So, to the clash of mighty weapons, the Trojan war is fought. The play, finally recorded, is a great success and wins a prize.

*   *   *

The first piece I ever wrote for actors was a short radio play called *The Dock Brief*, which grew up to be staged in the theatre, become a television play and then a film. Years ago, I sat in a state of high excitement and stared through a glass wall, like a visitor at an aquarium, at Michael Hordern and David Kossoff reading my lines out in a studio. There was no suggestion of going on location then. Now I have written another radio play called, like this book, *The Summer of a Dormouse*. The great advantage of these dramas is that you can get almost any actor you care to mention, because the reading only takes a few days and they don't have to learn the words. So, as I sit once again gazing at the fish tank, in which a girl is slopping water in a blue plastic washing-up bowl to simulate the waves of the sea, I can see Paul Scofield and Alex Jennings, Joanna David, Gemma Jones and Imelda Staunton, stars you might have great difficulty in getting to come out at night, learn the words and act in a theatre.

It's a play about growing old and being obsessed with Byron and his letters and journals. 'When one subtracts from life,' he wrote, 'infancy (which is vegetation), sleep,

124

eating and swilling, buttoning and unbuttoning—how much remains of downright existence? The summer of a dormouse.'

Byron's life, that of a revolutionary conservative, a down-to-earth romantic and a puritanical libertine, is a catalogue of glorious contradictions. Many writers invent their personalities, identities they assume as though they were fictional characters. Dickens invented himself as a commonsensical, decent, home-loving family man, although he was an unfaithful husband capable of elaborate deception. Evelyn Waugh invented himself as a grumpy and hard-drinking, reactionary, country squire and, in spite of his genius, grew into the part. Oscar Wilde, a man of huge kindness and good sense, did his best to act the part of an amoral aesthete. The popular invention of Byron as a doomed spirit, cursed with beauty and born to damnation, was one which he continually punctured, writing the greatest comic satire in the language and calling his finest lyrics 'poeshie'.

The ground floor of his Palazzo in Venice, which smelled of the sea, was given over to his coaches and a collection of animals, wrongly thought of as pets, which included a fox and a wolf, monkeys, birds of all sorts and Mutz, a ferocious Swiss mastiff who was once put to flight by a pig in the Apennines. On the *piano nobile*, up a marble staircase, was a huge empty billiard room and the bedroom, where Byron entertained his Venetian mistresses—including the little 'Bacchante', the peasant girl he had picked up on his afternoon ride, or Fornarina, his black-eyed tigress of a housekeeper with a violently jealous disposition. She often waited, furious, in the driving rain and darkness, for his gondola to return from an assignation on the Lido. Byron, who had more lovers, scandals and triumphs than most of us have had common colds, who rattled through Europe in a great lurching coach with his silver cutlery and his private doctor, who went off to fight for freedom in a huge helmet designed by himself on the lines of the one described in the sixth book of the Iliad, who died, bled by leeches, in his great four-poster in Missolonghi, thought of his life merely as the summer of a dormouse. So who am I to argue about that?

*   *   *

'I've got Peers of the Realm up to here! They think they can get into the House of Lords tomorrow. Most of them haven't got a clue. Thank God for a Knight!'

I am in the College of Heralds, a beautiful but somewhat run-down building in Queen Victoria Street. I have been admitted to the presence of Garter King at Arms, the Boss, the Chief Herald, generally know as 'Garter' for short. By my standards he is young, and dressed in a tweed suit, which gives him the air of a country gent off to the races. I have come to sign on.

'It's a perfectly simple process,' Garter assures me. 'Remember what we had at school? Bottle of ink. Dip-in pen. Although, at school, the bottle of ink was always bunged up with chewing gum and blotting paper, wasn't it? No chewing gum here. No blotch. Just dip your pen in and sign the book! You can manage that, can't you?'

I can manage it. As I sign my name I say, 'Is that all?'

'That's all. Unless you'd like a coat of arms.'

I think it over. 'Well, I'd quite like a coat of arms.' Something to emblazon, perhaps, on the car's mud-stained door?

'If you want a coat of arms,' Garter becomes unusually serious, 'choose a nice animal. Look at this fellow!' He pulls a huge book off a shelf and flicks through a collection of crests. 'Some bloody judge. See what he wanted? A woman's legs, on his coat of arms! Disgusting! Barbra Streisand's legs! Take my tip. Choose a nice animal.'

So I choose my animal, and a motto in Latin—AESTAS GLIRIS, 'The Summer of a Dormouse'.

CHAPTER TWELVE

'Jack Straw's coming, so why don't you have a go at him?' Hell Fire Corner, the name of Barbara Castle's house at Ibstone, across the valley, is appropriate. Still beautiful, her flaming hair paled, her clear blue eyes almost sightless, at eighty-nine Barbara is still bursting with conviction and able, with an oratory no one can equal, to give appropriate hell to the leaders of New Labour. She is Old Labour refusing to grow old, brushing aside such minor inconveniences as blindness and filled with the political passion which is now looked upon, from the high peaks of Government, as some sort of dangerous eccentricity.

Jack Straw was her protégé when she was Minister of Transport and has inherited her Blackburn constituency, so he and his wife are coming to lunch at Hell Fire Corner, down a perilous flight of steps from the road, negotiated each night by Barbara when she comes home from the House of Lords. We sit at lunch and drink Chilean wine and Barbara nudges me, 'Now then! It's time you had a go at Jack.'

It's difficult to have a go at someone sitting opposite you on a sunny Sunday, who is smiling charmingly (it's important to remember that no politician can achieve any sort of success without charm). Mr Straw also seems a modest sort of person, once the firebrand head of the Students' Union, now cooled off, bothered and embarrassed by his bodyguard. However, I do have serious concerns. The Labour Home Secretary seems cheerfully prepared to ignore Magna Carta, dangerously restrict jury trials and take a further damaging swipe at the presumption of innocence. Are these, or are they not, topics about which to bother a man as he digests his roast beef? I might have behaved myself and kept quiet had not Barbara, grinning at the delightful prospect of an argument, repeated, 'Now then. Have a really good go!'

It's not the first time that I've tested Jack Straw on the question of our civil liberties and the protection of the innocent. Before the Election, we met for another lunch, in the offices of the *New Statesman*. It was then that Jack said he regarded himself as a 'shop steward' for the electors of Blackburn, who might, indeed, not have any strong feelings about the presumption of innocence. I told him that although he was saying the sort of things about juries and civil rights that emerged from the then Conservative Home Secretary Michael Howard (under whose regime women prisoners were chained to their beds while giving birth), we all realized that such pronouncements were only there for the purpose of acquiring Conservative votes, and once the Election was over more sensible and constitutionally respectable policies would prevail. I told him that, as we all realized that it would be embarrassing to him to admit this in so many words, he would have a minute's silence during which he would be expected to wink. If he did so we would go away happy. A minute then passed in the *New Statesman* office, but Jack Straw didn't flutter an eyelid.

Not to disappoint Barbara, I put my toe in the murky water of rape cases. Under Jack Straw's new proposals, a man accused of rape will be forced to employ a lawyer to defend him and will not be allowed to conduct his own case. His ability to cross-examine will be seriously restricted, not by the judge, who can always stop questions which he considers irrelevant, but by the power of Parliament, which will censor cross-examination, regardless of the facts of a particular case. Rape is, no doubt, a terrible crime, to some people as serious as murder; but if you're accused of murder you can still appear in person and your right to cross-examine is not restricted by law.

'You're assuming that anyone accused of rape is guilty at the outset,' I challenged Jack. 'So he has to employ a lawyer and can't ask the sort of questions which might be permissible in a murder trial, or any other case. And so you've decided before the trial starts, that his accuser is telling the truth and the only point of his questions is to embarrass her. That means you're reversing the presumption of innocence.'

'You lawyers!' Mr Straw started off on a familiar road. It's the way of all politicians who seek to interfere in various areas, about which they are uninformed, to rubbish those who work in them daily; so they start a blast on education by announcing that all schoolteachers are undisciplined relics of the sixties, or deal with the countryside by alleging that the place is full of over-privileged toffs and useless, whinging farmers. Any lawyer who argues for civil rights and hard-won principles of justice is a money-grabbing fat cat who wants to prolong trials and might even get people off. One ex-QC, a brilliant criminal lawyer, was told that his views on jury trials were worth nothing because he lived in Hampstead.

'You lawyers,' Jack Straw repeated, smiling patiently at the antics of such a clearly corrupt class of persons, although he was a law student who was once called to the Bar, 'you want to blacken the character of some unfortunate woman and yet you keep all the details of your client's past a secret from the jury!'

Scenting some small victory, I asked, 'Didn't they tell you this before the Bar exams? If you attack the character of a prosecution witness, you let in all the details of your own client's character. The jury hears them and the prosecutor can cross-examine on them.'

'Oh, well,' Mr Straw's smile was charmingly modest, 'I suppose I'd forgotten that.'

On such a wealth of information are Government Bills put forward, I thought, and felt quite pleased with myself until I heard Barbara say, 'Well, you didn't have much of a go at Jack, did you now? I must say I expected better than that.'

*   *   *

If the Government wanted to produce a simple piece of decent legislation that wouldn't transgress Magna Carta or the Bill of Rights, how about a law requiring all restaurant lavatories to be on the ground floor? Those approaching early signs of autumn at the end of the dormouse summer rise unsteadily after half a bottle of wine and are directed to a narrow, twisting and ill-lit stairway, leading down to the murky dungeons in which the Ladies and Gents are confined. So the slow and painful journey begins, grabbing a weak rail, plotting a course with a wandering stick, towards distant relief at the buried porcelain. If you are sitting at lunch with a man who can remember the Blitz, and he suddenly looks thoughtful and abstracted, as though in touch with the Spirit of the Universe or about to declare undying love, he is only trying to decide whether to risk his neck down a horrible staircase or face public humiliation as the sweet trolley comes round.

But there's no limit to the mercy of strangers. I go into a new restaurant in Covent Garden and, as I'm early, ask for the loo. The black-suited, dark-haired manageress says, 'It's down fifty steps. You'll hate that. Can you hang on for five minutes?' 'Just about.' She makes a phone call and then says, 'It's all right. It's only half past twelve but they'll open it up for you.' So we set off, arm in arm, thank God on the level, to the Lyceum Theatre, where Henry Irving acted and Bram Stoker, his manager, wrote Dracula, modelled on the leading, cadaverous, self-absorbed star. As we arrive the doors are being unlocked and the ground-floor 'disabled' loo in the foyer is put at my disposal.

Stairs aren't the only deterrent to the growing weakness of the bladder. I was invited to speak to a gathering of judges and lawyers in Tampa. I was sent, in enormous luxury, to Miami, flying in one of British Airways' ingenious cabins in which you can join opposing seats to make a bed and erect a small partition to shut off the snores or gasps of love from fellow travellers. At Miami, I was met by a judge who ushered me through passport control and led me to a black stretch limo with darkened windows. Standing at the car's open back door was my driver, Mr Sanchez. Handsome, bearded, middle aged, he looked like an El Greco portrait and was wearing, in the blinding sunlight of a Florida afternoon, a dinner jacket with a neat black bow tie and a stand-up collar. He admitted me to the back of the stretch, which was well supplied with Diet Coke and Seven-Up, and we set off on the three-hour drive to Tampa.

We were crossing the Everglades, discussing the total disappearance of an aeroplane in the surrounding bog, when I broke the news to Mr Sanchez that I wanted urgently to pee.

'There's a good restaurant twenty miles on,' said Mr Sanchez. 'They'll have a nice clean restroom.'

'Mr Sanchez, twenty miles on is of no interest to me. If you wouldn't mind stopping for three minutes I'll get out here.'

The road looked empty as far as the eye could reach. The stretch limo purred to a stop. Mr Sanchez, in his dinner jacket, got out, threw open the door and bowed. I stepped on to the grass verge.

'By the way, Mr Sanchez,' I asked before I got down to business, 'what are those black things that look like a pile of spare tyres by the side of the road up there?'

'Those, sir,' Mr Sanchez was as calm and polite as ever, 'are alligators.'

I pulled up the zip and dived back into the car, ready to face a painful twenty-mile drive to the restroom.

                    *   *   *

On 1 May 1997, when we danced and cheered the night away in the Festival Hall and greeted our Leader when he descended from the skies with unstinted enthusiasm, we never guessed that, whatever politics would be like in the Labour Government we had waited so long for, they would simply become dull.

In an effort to awaken the electorate from its torpor, the Chancellor, Gordon Brown, has launched an attack on Oxford University, alleging it favours the entry of students from fee-paying schools over those who were educated by the State. I'm not sure this is true, and I know that Etonians often find it difficult to get into the older universities. Gordon Brown's intervention has failed to do anything as exciting as reviving the class war; perhaps a difficult trick to pull off with a Prime Minister who went to a public school and Oxford; and I have to say that I've never found my public-school experience, mildly unpleasant at the time, of the slightest help to me in any career.

I am leaving my house to go to London and at the end of the track I find a chimney-sweep's van waiting. I remember that we'd made some arrangement about our chimneys, so I stop to speak to the sweep, a cheerful-looking, middle-aged man who is reading the *Daily Telegraph* and eating a sandwich. I ask him if he is coming to our house. 'No,' he says.

135

'But I am an excellent sweep. I advertise in the parish magazine and it would be a pleasure to look after your chimneys at any time.' I tell him I'll remember him and, as he gives me his card, he says, 'Harrow didn't do much for either of us, did it?'

When I look back to those days in wartime Harrow, with distant London lit up by the Blitz, gas masks and fagging, I remember the head boy, Hugh Derwent. He was extremely handsome, was Derwent, excellent at Classics and brilliant at cricket. How would he end up after we had won the war? Prime Minister would hardly be enough for him.

Twenty years later, I was having dinner in Hollywood when a quiet, upper-class English voice murmured solicitously in my right ear, 'New potatoes and green beans, sir?' I looked round to see Hugh Derwent, the boy most likely to succeed, wearing a tail coat and following the no-doubt lucrative career of an English butler in Tinseltown.

When I started to write plays, it was the era of *Room at the Top*, *Look Back in Anger* and *Saturday Night and Sunday Morning*. Successful writers had gritty northern accents, or at least came from acceptably underprivileged backgrounds. Girls from Cheltenham Ladies College and boys from Westminster were desperately flattening their vowels and doing their best to acquire classless accents like Albert Finney or Rita Tushingham. To have admitted to Harrow would have been a social and professional disaster, the equivalent of admitting you are a socialist at a New Labour Party conference. Now, at the start of the millennium, information technology is whisking us back to the social world of the early P. G. Wodehouse but, sadly, without the jokes.

The chimney-sweep is now attacking our chimneys with great energy and skill. He says our meeting will be a good subject for his speech at the next Old Harrovian dinner.

*   *   *

The battle of Hendrickje Stoffels' pudenda. There is a debate between three *New Yorker* writers and three contributors to the *Independent* in England. The subject for discussion is whether American culture will dominate the world in the new millennium. The contest is staged in Cheltenham Ladies College and I am the Chairman and meant to keep some sort of order.

On the English team is Howard Jacobson, a good novelist and funny speaker. The Americans have enlisted Simon Schama who, though brought up in Golders Green, now lives in New York and is Professor of Art History at Columbia. His latest book is a marvellously written and lavishly illustrated study of Rembrandt. Hendrickje Stoffels, according to Schama, was the painter's mistress and gave birth to his daughter. A few months before the birth, she received a lengthy public rebuke as she stood before the Church Council. She was informed of her depravity, and denounced for prostituting herself to the infamous Rembrandt. He had to suffer no such humiliation and painted her several times, most notably in a work known as 'Hendrickje Bathing in a River', which now hangs in the National Gallery. In this picture, she is shown standing in dark water, holding up her shift and looking downwards. A detailed study shows some faint reflection in the water, which comes about halfway up Hendrickje's calves.

It is this picture, and the accompanying text, which causes Howard Jacobson to tell the audience that they can't accept a single word spoken by Schama, because he suggests that what Hendrickje was doing was staring at her pudenda reflected in the stream. This is such a ridiculous suggestion, Jacobson argues, that its author must be totally unreliable. From then on, the future of American culture is largely forgotten. A furious argument centres round what Rembrandt's mistress could see, and why she is looking downwards.

Those who have seen the picture will remember Hendrickje. She is broad shouldered, solid, her arms and hands are workmanlike. She is firmly raising her shift to show strong thighs and knees used to scrubbing floors as well as bending in church. But her features are delicate, her dark eyes heavy lidded as they gaze gently downwards. She is a real woman, full bodied and alive, not only desirable but beautiful. So what is she doing exactly? This is what Schama says in his book: 'More likely, though, Hendrickje is looking, the suggestion of a smile playing about her lips, into the watery mirror of her own reflected body, privy to a view denied us, and emphatically obscured by the black depth of that shadow below her shift.'

So is she examining the reflection of her pudenda, or is Schama only suggesting that we might examine the possibility that she is doing so, which is how one debater explained the passage. Who can tell? All I can do, in summing up the arguments for and against American culture, is to advise the voters to exclude Hendrickje's pudenda from their minds. Of course they could, once safely home, before going to bed stand in a bath which came halfway up their calves, to find out what, if anything, they could see reflected. I have no means of knowing how many tried this experiment.

CHAPTER THIRTEEN

It's the time ahead that's the worry. Not only the frequent occurrence of breakfast, the days chasing each other like Keystone Cops at the end of an old movie or Benny Hill after girls. It's not the bother of walking with a stick—this comes as naturally as running in childhood— it's not the time spent planning how to get to your feet, or the need to persuade those around you to sit on chairs to stop them falling over when you grab them as an aid to standing. It's not even that you may be compelled, in the not-too-distant future, to write off for the 'Adjustable Urinal' ('Secure, yet comfortable to wear like an athlete's support'), the 'Practical Bath Seat', the 'Gentle Pelvic Exerciser', the 'Complete Video Guide to Manageable Sex Over Sixty', or even the 'Decorative Sticker Window Films' to stop you walking into glass doors. (I have to say I have done without these helpful articles so far.) The real trouble with old age is that it lasts for such a short time.

All worthwhile projects are investments in the future. It takes years to grow a tree to any size, it can take a long time to get a film produced or a play put on, a year to write a novel and another year to see it published. After you're seventy, it's probably too late to establish another career, create a mature garden, or discover a new way of writing. The old, grabbing time by the forelock, have to go for immediate results.

Worst of all, there's not time to see a child grow up. Men who become fathers after sixty may not be at their children's twenty-first birthday parties. So should there be a law against it? Is being an old father intolerably selfish? A woman of fifty who wanted *in vitro* fertilization was denied it because she was considered too old, although she might have had twenty-five years or more with her child. Yet today, a sixty-seven-year-old grandfather writes cheerfully about changing nappies for his own newborn baby. Is it completely out of the question to have a child who may, when barely ten years old, have to dress up for his or her father's funeral? For me life becomes insupportable, and inoperable pomposity is liable to set in, unless there's a fairly young child about the place. Having such a child makes it essential not to die until it's absolutely necessary.

I was sixty-two when Rosie was born and I mean to enjoy her company as long as possible. She shows disturbing signs of having the character of a novelist. When she was very young, we were having a bath together (a fact which would lead to our immediate arrest if known to the Social Workers) and she suddenly said, 'I don't love you, Dad.' 'That's very sad,' I told her. 'Yes,' Rosie admitted. 'It's sad but it is interesting.' This weekend, on her way back to school, she told Penny about her conversation with the man who drives them to the dentist. When he asks about her family, she says that her mother is a secretary and her father a supply teacher.

On an aeroplane, she was asked by the woman in the next seat why she was coming back from Italy alone. She told an apparently convincing story about her grandmother having died on holiday, so she was going back to collect her eight brothers and sisters and take them out to the funeral. She said she was the only one who went to a private school, because her uncle died and left her enough money in his will. As she lives in this rich fantasy world, I hope she won't be too upset by the death of the supply teacher.

*   *   *

New Labour has not formed a Government that welcomes criticism, and I have no ambitions for public office. I have, however, quite unexpectedly been given a job which is time consuming, quite unprofitable and will, no doubt, end in a whirlwind of public anger, disappointment and abuse. Chris Smith, the Secretary of State for Culture, has made me Lord of the Plinth. 'The plinth of darkness,' some civil servant with a taste for puns, who was soon promoted away from his job, said.

It's also the plinth of emptiness, because my plinth, the plinth over whose fortune I may, just possibly, have some influence, which has got on its shiny roseate surface a space large enough to contain a horse and rider or a group of all-in wrestlers, has nothing on it whatever.

Trafalgar Square, they say, is at the heart of London, as Times Square is in New York or the Eiffel Tower in Paris. It's where people go to get drunk on New Year's Eve, or jump in the fountains during a heat wave, or take their children to feed the pigeons. It's also where they go to protest, about the Poll Tax or Suez or the Vietnam War or whatever needs protesting about at the time. It's where playwrights such as Arnold Wesker and Robert Bolt sat down in support of Nuclear Disarmament. The setting for those radical demonstrations is a square dedicated to the triumphs of our imperial past.

On a column high as the masts of his ships, Admiral Nelson, hero and adulterer, is isolated among the pigeons and near to the clouds. In front of him, secure on their plinths, are two generals who fought in India for the British Raj. On one side, wearing a heavy cloak thrown back, with one hand grasping a sword and the other a scroll, is General Sir Charles Napier. He is remembered, if at all, for one small joke. When he captured the Indian city of Scinde, he sent a message back to the War Office which contained just one word, 'Peccavi'—Latin for 'I have sinned'. Next to him is Major General Sir Henry Havelock, hero of the Indian campaign of 1857. He is standing bare headed, with one hand on his grounded sword, the other inserted in his belt. The inscription on his plinth reads: 'Soldiers. Your labour, your privations, your sufferings and your valour will not be forgotten by a grateful country. H. Havelock.' In front of these statues, long haired and seated on an elegant horse, Charles I looks down Whitehall towards the place of his execution. Guarding Nelson crouch four lions, cast in bronze and designed by the Victorian painter Sir Edwin Landseer. These lions have unnervingly human qualities. Although they were cast from the 'anatomical lion' preserved in Turin, they look like aged and shifty politicians.

Behind Nelson, nearer to the National Gallery end of the square, there are two more plinths. On one, riding a horse, is George IV, once the Prince Regent who secretly married Mrs Fitzherbert and got rid of his wife Queen Caroline in a sensational divorce case. Next to him is the problem that has become mine, the empty fourth plinth.

The square once housed the King's Mews, where the Royal horses and hawks were kept and Chaucer was 'Clerk of the Mews'. It became in turn a barracks for the

Parliamentary army, where four-and-a-half thousand Cavalier prisoners were confined during the Civil War, a menagerie, and a place where public records were stored. In 1840, Sir Charles Barry started to build the present square but, with the fourth plinth still untenanted, the money ran out. A few years ago, Prue Leith, restaurateur, caterer and novelist, and Deputy Chairman of the Royal Society of Arts, drove round the square, noticed the desert island of a plinth and decided she'd try to do something about it. Being a woman of great drive and tenacity, she succeeded, and three works by contemporary artists were made to occupy the plinth in turn, until a permanent solution could be found.

I go and look at the plinth. The buses are stacked up between it and the National Gallery, cars are changing lanes, trying to spot an opening and win a clear run round the square. A pigeon is sitting on George IV's head, school parties from Germany, Norway and High Wycombe are sitting on the steps and leaning on the railings of the National Gallery. In the church of St Martin in the Fields, the square's finest piece of architecture, there are washing machines, chiropodists and an advice centre for those who sleep in doorways or under arches in the favoured area between Lincoln's Inn Fields and the river.

Tonight some of them will be bedding down

near George Washington's statue on a patch of grass outside the gallery. On the pedestal of Nelson's column there is a bas-relief depicting the Battle of Trafalgar and the message 'England expects every man to do his duty.' I must try and think who ought to be on the committee of the plinth.

*   *   *

Thinking about leaving children as a gesture of immortality, no one has gone about it more thoroughly than Joss Ackland, who has seven children and twenty-nine grandchildren. What I love about Joss, apart from the splendour of his acting, is the cheerfulness with which he and Rosemary greet the disasters which punctuate their lives. One New Year's Eve, Rosemary was knocked down on a pedestrian crossing in Paris and was taken to hospital, where the doctor appeared wearing a blond wig and an enormous pair of false tits. He blamed the Acklands for having dragged him away from a party. Joss also gave me an account of their journey to Sicily, which he could hardly tell for laughing. They put their car on a train from Milan and it was broken into during the night and their luggage stolen. After a number of adventures which led to frequent phone calls to the AA, they arrived in Sicily during a dramatic thunderstorm. Rosemary was driving and the rain-soaked

146

road caused the car to skid and crash through a huge hoarding advertising babies' nappies. They landed in a ploughed field. Extricating himself, Joss stumbled back to the road, where he found a wayside phone and started, once again, to call the AA. Before he could get through, however, the telephone was struck by lightning and, as he remembered with delight, melted in his hand.

Large and cheerful, Joss was born to play Falstaff and Captain Shotover. I wanted him to be in a revival of *Voyage Round My Father*, and telephoned him when he was staying, for another film, in some Italian hotel. He answered my call calmly and cheerfully enough, but there were sounds of high drama, shouts, screams and hammering on doors, to be heard in the background. I interrupted a conversation about possible touring dates to ask what the hell was going on. One of Joss's daughters, it seemed, had got a job on the production, and the Italian boyfriend to whom she had given the boot was on the stairs and hammering to get in. 'It's a bit more complicated than that,' Joss chuckled. 'You see, he was given money by the Italian police to buy drugs so they could identify and arrest the dealers. Unfortunately he spent the money and never gave them any information. So the police are out there too.'

Last night we went to Joss's party, but as he was born on 29 February, it is not his seventy-second but only his eighteenth birthday. I left feeling envious of his youth and the marvellous events which follow wherever he goes— situations to make a writer jealous.

*　　　*　　　*

Lunch with Tabitha. We talk about her near-perfect upbringing. With an Irish nurse for her mother and a diplomat for her father, she was adopted at birth by the vicar of a Warwickshire parish and his wife. Shortly after the adoption, the vicar's wife decamped to Spain with the parish clerk and Tabby was left with the vicar as her single parent. She walked to school in a village that had until then never seen a black child. She sat under her surrogate father's desk while he was writing his sermons. In his care, she eventually got a scholarship to the London School of Economics, followed by a degree in philosophy and a job in BBC documentaries, and wrote a book on the Boer War. Now her father is certainly the vicar; she loves him and shows him London during his frequent visits.

The whole situation would be anathema to social workers nowadays, who would have shoved Tabby into some family who had suffered racial abuse, and would have been appalled at a small girl being cared for, and loved, by a single white vicar. Fortunately, the social workers stayed away and Tabby has grown up to be what she is, a girl with her roots in the Church of England and the English countryside. She says she's going to leave the BBC for a while to fulfil her great ambition, which is to write a history of facial hair, finding, as she does, the comings and goings of moustaches and mutton-chop whiskers sublimely entertaining.

*   *   *

The first of Prue Leith's temporary exhibits has gone on the plinth. *Ecce Homo*, a white life-sized statuette of Christ, crowned with thorns and with his hands tied behind his back. Isolated on the plinth, and lonely as Jesus brought before Pilate, it's a moving piece of work by Mark Wallinger, and it arouses considerable interest and general approval. I discover that sculpture today is not the tedious business of chiselling at marble or modelling in clay which caused Michelangelo and Rodin so much trouble. Mark Wallinger's Jesus is basically a friend, who allowed himself to be put in plaster and was liberated when the work was cast. The artist who made the Angel of the North, it seems, went through the same process, with straw in his nose so he could breathe while being cast as an angel. I have an old-fashioned feeling that art should be more difficult, but Wallinger's conception, the idea of a small, pale God facing a horrible death, provides a startling contrast to the dark lions

149

and imperial heroes with which he is surrounded.

If the plinth is still short of a permanent tenant, at least it has a committee. I managed to persuade Ruth Rendell, most brilliant of writers and assiduous member of the House of Lords, to join, and we have Neil MacGregor, Director of the National Gallery, Richard Cork, *The Times* art critic, Peter Clarke, the Cambridge historian, Elsie Owusu, a successful architect, and Bob Harris, a Labour Councillor from Greenwich. None of us, I'm sure, would be prepared to put straws up our noses, be covered in plaster, cast and erected on the plinth.

I have lunch before the first plinth meeting with Kathy Lette, which is always a treat. Kathy is one of four sisters, the eldest of whom is a sergeant in the Sydney police. Her father, Mervyn, worked in optical fibres and is known to the family as 'Optic Merv' in a habit of punning which Kathy has carried on in her book titles, such as *Foetal Attraction*. At lunch we exchange what Australians know as 'the goss'. Then Kathy tells me she has taken part in a programme of readings by women writers under the title 'Vagina Monologues'. This performance was given at the Old Vic and after it there was a party for the readers and selected members of the audience. For the event, someone had baked a cake in the shape of a massive vagina, but understandably, as some of the readings had dealt with the outrage of female circumcision, no one was prepared to take a knife to it. The cake was never cut, but furtively crumbled round the edges.

I do my best to dismiss this strange image from my mind and set out for the Department for Culture, Media and Sport in Cockspur Street, to face the question of who or what should stand beside Nelson in Trafalgar Square.

CHAPTER FOURTEEN

The ends of eras, also perhaps the ends of lives, provide useful soil for superstition. Magic and mysteries and the excessive reliance on soothsayers, fortune-tellers and dissectors of entrails marked the decline of the Roman Empire. After the First World War, even such a sensible, down-to-earth and rational figure as Conan Doyle ended his life not only in frequent communication with the spirit world, but with a firm belief in fairies. Now our neighbours in this corner of the Chiltern hills are divided about the magical health-giving properties of a small black box shaped like the television's remote-control.

Friends of ours in Hungerford were introduced to black boxes by a local doctor, who has them imported from Russia. The theory is very like acupuncture but, as the Russians are short of clean or reliable needles, a succession of small electric shocks emitted from the black box take their place. Application of this device to affected spots, the news spreads around the countryside, will cause eczema and other skin complaints to vanish, patches of hard skin to soften and arthritic joints to become more mobile. Even cancer patients, it's rumoured, achieve a remarkable remission after regular doses of the black box. This was news I greeted with the cynicism of someone with only a tentative faith in conventional doctors—and very little in alternative forms of medicine.

No one knows much about leg ulcers, these red badges of old age, but everyone you ask has a different theory. So I have tried all sorts of dressings and ointments. I have been advised to go to bed for a month, I have been told that such a course would have fatal results, but nothing has made much difference. Then the doctor rang and said there were two girls living near who were experts in the black box, and Penny persuaded me to have a try.

I hear them laughing and two heads of bright blonde hair in Afro curls bob past the windows. They come in spreading out their arms and generous with their kisses. They are identical twins, Vicky and Jackie, married to two members of the rock group Deep Purple.

Like heavenly twins, they are dressed in white clothing, some of it floating, other bits clinging tightly to them. They sink to the floor, one of them crawls under my desk and they apply the black box to the wounded leg. They are elegantly suntanned, remarkably pretty and speak with traces of a Birmingham accent.

I set out to learn more about them. Their father was a successful butcher near Walsall, who bought a Country Club where various pop stars came to stay. They were known as the Gibbs Twins and were the sensation of the Speak Easy Club in London in the seventies. They performed, for a while, in a small theatre in Rome. Vicky married Jon Lord of Deep Purple and the wedding party was held at the Country Club, and so Jackie met Ian Paice of the same group and they got married too. They have always been, they say, 'interested in healing'. I have a few bad moments when I learn that they polish people's auras, but such doubts disappear in the pleasure of their company. They are happy survivors from a vanished age and a gentler youth culture; at home they sit on bean-bags in front of log fires and look at crystals. They inhabit grand houses with billiard rooms and bring me presents— flowers, socks or organic champagne. Their visits, as they kneel by my feet or wriggle under the desk, turn easily into party nights. These social events are presided over and carefully monitored by Liz, a State Registered Nurse and expert practitioner of conventional medicine. She's there to change the dressings and see if she can find any improvement in my leg.

The irritating thing is that she can. The biggest wound is changing shape, getting smaller, and there are signs of young skin. My comfortable cynicism is turning to reluctant belief. The heavenly twins are not only good company, they are producing distinct signs of healing, which is extremely disconcerting. Up till now I had thought of them only as the positive side of leg ulcers.

*   *   *

Terry brings the letters early, before breakfast—when he is off duty they tend to sidle up at lunch-time. There's a big bundle kept together by two elastic bands; many of them are letters from strangers. These strangers write to me about their legal or their literary problems and ask for advice which I am little qualified to give. One letter combined both subjects. 'I think you might like to know that our sister has just murdered our mother. Do you think that this would make a good plot for a television play?'

Now I open sheets of neat, familiar handwriting with no address, signed only with the letter T. I have never met T, but she has been writing to me for years, about the wonderful times we had together last weekend, and 'Didn't Denise and Ken look daggers when they saw us walk into the pub together,' or how tired, indeed drained I looked when she spotted me going round Hyde Park in a car. 'You really must be careful.' T's letters usually end with another assignation. 'All right then, if you insist. Platform Three, Paddington Station at the usual time.' I am grateful for these letters and the alternative existence they have granted me, and wonder what I have been up to this time.

T apologizes for not having been more alert yesterday. She lets me know that she is going to sing the Fauré Requiem on the fourteenth of March, so maybe we'll have to wait until Ron's holiday on the eighteenth. She also wonders if I ever met anyone from Oundle, although she feels, instinctively, that I wouldn't have. It is, in a way, one of the most challenging and interesting of her letters. What would have happened at the Fauré Requiem if Ron hadn't been around at the time? Would I have been expected to sing? Who is Ron anyway, where's he going, and do we creep into his flat when he's off in Parakeet Bay? I do my very best to remember if I've ever met anyone from Oundle. For a moment I long to enter the world of Fauré and Ron. Should I hang about all day on Platform Three, at Paddington? But T's world is as intangible as a dream, so I open another letter, which is this time from an animal-rights stranger hoping I die of an incurable disease. It's signed, quite simply, 'A Well Wisher'.

*   *   *

There is no subject more productive of comic relief than politicians discussing morality. At the moment they are all prodigiously excited about whether to preserve the mysterious Clause 28, a law which prevents local authorities allowing their schools to tell children that homosexual relationships are as good as marriage. As always, politicians are extolling the virtues of 'family life', which can be a bed of delights or, as readers of Greek drama, Shakespeare, the Bible and the *News of the World* well know, a fruitful seed-bed for murder, incest, sadistic cruelty and pathetic marital deceit. Which is more moral, a marriage in which the drunken father beats the wife and sexually assaults the children, or the loving home and long relationship of a gay couple living with two long-haired terriers in Guildford?

The other fact of life that politicians haven't noticed is that teaching morality, or politically correct behaviour, in schools should be calculated to have an entirely opposite effect from the one intended. Throughout my childhood in the thirties I went to schools where I was told the British Empire was a

156

glorious institution, that death in war was a heroic conclusion to anyone's life and that, on the whole, the Conservative Party, led by Baldwin and Neville Chamberlain, was a good thing. The inevitable result of such teaching was that I became a pacifist and a one-boy Communist cell at Harrow. If the politicians who love Section 28 still believe that your sexual preferences are a matter of choice, they should repeal it at once and ensure that all schoolboys see endless videos showing how Dan and Roger bring up little Kevin in a committed relationship. There might then be a rush to heterosexual love.

We who lived through English pre-war, middle-class education in single-sex preparatory and so-called public schools, needed no laws abolished to introduce us to the gay world. It was as much a part of the syllabus as cold showers, muddy football fields and chapel before breakfast. I've been to visit an old friend, Toby, who lives in a fine Georgian house and has a pond full of trout in his garden. We were talking about the prep school we both went to, where Toby was younger than me and considerably better looking. 'The place was all right,' he told me for the first time, 'but Bingo Ollard [who taught us French and History] was always kissing me. Actually I went and told the Headmaster about it.'

'Oh yes. And what did he say?'

'Well,' he said, 'Do understand, Mr Ollard is what we call a homosexual, which means he likes boys better than girls. And if you look around you'll find that most of the masters in place are homosexual, or why else would they take on the job? The pay's not much and you boys can be extremely irritating. I'd like you to remember that, and if Mr Ollard kisses you again, just let me know!'

All this was a long time ago and Toby's grandchildren go to the same school now, undeterred by the Eloïse and Abelard relationship between Mr Bingo Ollard and their grandfather.

*   *   *

Terrible things are happenings in Mozambique. The country is inundated, no, drowned in water. Families are taking refuge on the roof-tops, on the pimple crests of hills, as the water rises. Children are strapped to branches by their belts and a woman has given birth in a tree-top before she and her baby are hauled to safety by a helicopter. It's all on the television. On the television also is an actor asking us all to send money to Mozambique.

I write a cheque, but I'm not sure where to send it and I have forgotten the name of the actor. I have forgotten his name and he's not only a famous actor but one of the most famous actors in the world. And he's not only one of the most famous actors in the world, but I have just written a part for him, or rather I have adapted Sancho Panza for him. This is the moment when, like King Lear, you stand in the middle of the room and shout 'Oh let me not be mad', or rather, 'For God's sake, don't say I've got Alzheimer's.' Are the gates creaking open to a dark garden where memories cease to exist?

Panic sets in, as it does when you empty your pockets at night and in the morning can't find your money, until it turns up, inexplicably, on top of the electric toaster, or when you hunt, with increasing desperation, for the book you were reading, or when you realize that the glasses you're looking for are, in fact, settled on your nose. What would it be like, in truth, to be released from all knowledge of the past? In such a state, is happiness possible?

John Piper, a prodigious painter and a man of many memories, living down in Fawley Bottom, entered the Alzheimer world years before he died and closed the door after him. He smiled a great deal and looked, as ever, like a white-haired, slim, handsome, hawk-faced ecclesiastic with an eye for the girls. But his studio was dusted and tidy, his canvases stacked against the walls, his brushes clean and his paints laid out in order. He produced no more pictures, and at lunch put his fork in his pocket and his pencil in the fish. His son, Edward, also a painter of talent, died of cancer, and John's wife Myfanwy couldn't tell John, or discuss it, or show her grief. But was he, behind that locked gate, contented? Had he mercifully forgotten that there was anything missing? He sat in our garden and I asked him if he was happy. He nodded as though with complete understanding and said, 'Yes. Very happy.'

And then a miracle happened. He went into his studio and took out his brushes, he mixed his paints, as always, on a sheet of glass, he stood a canvas on the easel and started to paint a picture. More than that, he finished it. It was a painting of the garden at Fawley Bottom. There was the path between the two borders, leading to the Gothic arch and the gate. The garden was in full flower, blue and pink and white, with peonies and irises and cornflowers and, here and there, herbs and vegetables. The sun was shining and it was a picture of his life at its best. I looked at it and remembered. It was an exact replica, a repeat of a picture he'd done twenty years before, reproduced in a book of his works, and this was only an echo, something left stranded on the beach after the sea had retreated.

So what's the actor's name? Bill something. No, Brian. No, not possible, try Ralph. As a barrister I started with will cases and divorce. The question, when it came to the validity of wills, was the testator's soundness of mind, memory and understanding. No one mentioned Alzheimer's then, it was all about arterial sclerosis, the hardening of the arteries, impeding the flow of nourishing blood to the brain. This condition led to the sufferer losing all memory of his friends and relations, except for those who were grouped round his bed persuading him to leave them his house and all the furniture. So that is how it ends, is it, staring, entranced, at the pattern of sunlight on a blanket, while a pen is stuck between your helpless fingers? I try remembering the name of the other actor in *Don Quixote*. '*Don Quixote*, with John Lithgow and . . .' There it is, lit up, like suddenly discovering a way out of a bewildering one-way system. BOB HOSKINS! Of course. Isn't it obvious? And an excellent name it is, too. A wonderfully apposite name. It fits him exactly. Everyone knows it and I can rejoin the great vocal majority. Madness is now a distant memory.

I only hope that when John Piper said he was happy with Alzheimer's he was telling the truth.

CHAPTER FIFTEEN

We're driving along the Harrow Road, a journey I took twenty-six years ago, up to the register office to marry Penny. I was in a long case at the Old Bailey when a juryman asked for a day off to go to his mother-in-law's funeral. So we booked the Harrow Road register office on that free day for our wedding.

Now, more than a quarter of a century later, I am in the car with Emily, going under the flyover towards the long road of pubs and electrical-accessory shops, down-at-heel bistros and supermarkets brilliantly lit in the middle of the afternoon. We are going to another Penelope, to whom Emily is not at all related, but she has come because her half-brother and half-sisters, and other remote members of her generation, have asked her to be there. We drive on and turn down narrower roadways, between trees and beside lawns, and stop in a gravel car-park where the half-sisters and the half-brother are getting out of cars with their smartened-up children, greeting each other as their husbands linger politely in the background. They talk quietly, gently, anxious not to surprise each other, and we all move slowly, but inevitably, towards the West London Crematorium.

It's hard to believe that so much talent, anger, humour, dash and desperation could be shut in a long and slender box which waits while her children read extracts from Penelope's *Garden Diary*, and while we sing 'For all the Saints, who from their labours rest,' and then listen to an Eddie Izzard tape. Sitting there, I can only remember the best of

162

times. The day I saw her kneeling in the garden of the cottage, when she was living with another lover, carefully painting his coal scuttle for the improvement of his home. The evenings when I walked through the woods and across the fields to visit her in Turville. The first time we went to Venice and our rich, gay host introduced us as the 'two penniless heterosexuals from Hampstead'. A winter in Spain when we had to get hold of two houses because there were so many children, and the matadors wore cloth caps and zipped jackets in the ring. The day Penelope met my mother, who later said she had 'very nice eyes for a divorced person'. Now Madelon is holding the quiet and awestruck Co-co, while she stands in the pulpit and reads further accounts of the garden her mother made in the Cotswolds. A woman is in charge, a young woman with a long black skirt and jacket and hat—half bowler, half top-hat—of the sort Winston Churchill once wore. There is a touch of dressage about her, of the control of delicately prancing horses; there is also, perhaps, a whiff of the circus. She makes a large, fluent gesture in front of the brass gates and Penelope slides out of sight.

So the family go away, back to the car-park, silent or reduced to whispers. The mere act of being alive seems somehow selfish, a cause of guilt. Some darkly dressed figures I haven't noticed have joined us: Penelope's friends, a journalist who is writing about her, Leslie Phillips, the actor, who was for a long time in love with Penelope's daughter, Caroline.

Back in the North London flat, the silence is broken, as though, in a moment, opening the wine and setting out the sandwiches, the whole family remembers that living is not necessarily a matter of guilt. The tall grandchildren, who don't often meet, exchange news and plans for an endless future where death is no part of the equation. And then, unaccompanied, Madelon and Caroline sing one of the songs Penelope and I wrote and played on pub pianos, a few years after the war. The lyrics are imitation Noel Coward in his Matelot era, but Penelope's tune is catchy:

'Limelight child, with clowns to care for you,
A mother to swing high up in the air for you,
Over the crowds to do and to dare for you . . .
Sleep till the morning comes.'

The time when we sang that seems near enough to touch.

*   *   *

Life after death will always be a subject for argument and conjecture, but one thing is certain, one post-mortem event is unavoidable: the sharing out of the furniture, the books taken off the shelves and divided, the lease of

164

the flat disposed of. I am glad to have been brought, by my daughter Sally, something useful to her mother and to me in our declining years. It's a lightweight metal walking stick which has, at its head, a handle with a lever which works a grasping, claw-like foot. With such a device you can sit in your chair and grab books, papers, rubbish, dropped glasses and even bottles in the middle distance, without rising from your seat. Penelope's clutching stick has a loop of tinsel round its handle, as though it was once a present for Christmas.

So, after so many years of love, adventure, rivalry, disputes and separation, we share the services of a stick with a claw for picking up the things we are too old, or too idle, to reach for.

CHAPTER SIXTEEN

Miracle of miracles. The Royal Court Theatre is finished, reborn, rebuilt, back in the land of the living, open armed, ready to receive plays. The traffic is circulating round Sloane Square again, people are sitting, as they always did, on the steps, reading books, waiting for their lovers or just staring into space. We have tucked our new restaurant underground and lights from the bar glow up by the theatre entrance. Run by a caterer aptly named Digby Trout, the restaurant has a staircase up to a sort of Metro exit in the middle of the square. We are not allowed to use this yet, in case people should emerge with drinks on summer evenings and sit round the paved patch looking unnecessarily cheerful. No doubt we shall win our planning permission in time.

We have a new theatre upstairs with great windows looking out over London, and dressing-rooms with tall windows, where actors can sleep and shower. We have a balcony outside the dress-circle bar where you can stand and look down towards King's Road. The auditorium is no larger than it ever was, and it feels as though we have come home to something much more beautiful than we remember. And as for the seats! Well, for a start, there are no black-leather dentist's chairs here. The seats are a pleasantly faded reddish brown, they are surprisingly comfortable, and in front of each one, there is a little net arranged like the pocket in front of an aeroplane chair, where you can put your shopping, your sandwiches, your copy of the Big Issue. Are they seats or benches? The wonder of it is they are both, or they could be either. Their arms can slide up or down, allowing optional thigh contact to those who want it or find themselves next to approachable thighs. The conception is symbolic of getting money for the Arts. Get yourself a seat next to the Arts Council or a business tycoon and quietly lower the intervening arm.

The theatre opens to universally good notices, the all-purpose, thrush-free seats being greeted as the stars of the show. There's a glass-fronted lift that climbs up the side of the building, and I glide up to Ian Rickson's office, which features the fashionably distressed stonework of the old theatre's wall. Stephen is there and we drink white wine and try to decide which was the most dramatic moment in the long rebuilding story. He and Ian agree it was when I told them to stop massaging their tenuous senses of morality. The restaurant is beautiful, the place booked out by an audience who want to see the theatre as well as the plays, and David Hare, all things forgiven, is writing a play for us. The immense relief is not so much relish for the building's success, but gratitude at having escaped disaster.

Now we're having a Royal visit. Princess Alexandra is there, and we've been told she doesn't like bad language. It might be thought unfortunate that Conor McPherson's new play is almost a monologue spoken by Brian Cox as a dipsomaniac Irish undertaker. Sitting next to the Princess, I wait nervously for the first 'fuck'. I don't have long to wait and I know there's a 'cunt' on page three of the script.

To her great credit, the Princess takes all

this on the chin, and the whole party spends at least half an hour afterwards talking enthusiastically to the actors.

In the bar, I'm talking to a grey-haired woman who discloses herself as Sean O'Casey's daughter, Shivaun. I remember that Harold Macmillan was best friends with O'Casey's widow, took her out regularly, and urgently proposed marriage to her after his wife died. All this seems to be a sign of a healthier political age, and it's now hard to imagine a one-time Tory Prime Minister wanting to marry the Communist widow of a Communist playwright. Shivaun tells me that her father liked his Conservative friends much better than his Communist friends, who were, she says, quite frankly a pain in the neck. His principle, apparently, was to vote with the Left but have dinner with the Right.

*   *   *

There's nothing so enjoyable as giving away other people's money, and at the Court we are giving away Pearson's bursaries to new writers and attaching them to theatres where they can work and learn their trade. Many successful writers have won these prizes in their time, including Sue Townsend, who is here, funny and cheerful, having lived through some horrible illness. Now she is almost blind, holding up a big magnifying glass like a windscreen between us. I remember hearing that her ex-husband was in a nervous and distressed state when he was taken by their children to see a psychiatrist in Leicester, where the family have always lived. After a prolonged interview behind a closed door, the psychiatrist came out to the children and said, in a muted voice of serious concern, 'I'm afraid your father is very ill indeed. He imagines he's married to Sue Townsend.'

This year's winner is Gary Mitchell, short, stocky, in his twenties, pale, with gingery hair and small, round glasses. He comes from a Belfast housing estate, left school when he was sixteen and was then unemployed for eight years, except for a short spell in a government office, where his only job was to fetch and carry files and he wasn't allowed to answer the telephone. His father is, it seems, a largely unemployed entertainer and his mother is a devout Protestant. Out of sheer boredom, he joined a local drama group and said he simply couldn't understand the characters in *Wozzeck*, the play they were rehearsing.

He wanted to know, for instance, exactly how many women his character was acquainted with. When the group were unable to tell him, he suggested that he write them a play about characters on a Belfast housing estate, which he could understand. When he did so, the drama group found it too close for comfort, so he sent it to BBC radio, where it was immediately accepted. Now his second play for the Court is being rehearsed and his ex-entertainer dad is very proud of his son in show business. His second play suggests a close collaboration between a member of the Royal Ulster Constabulary and Protestant terrorists, and should provoke outrage and admiration.

Sue Townsend, who has been out on the theatre's new balcony to smoke a fag, is leaving with a thin, smiling grey-haired man 'to help him with his novel set in a gay retirement home'. I feel suddenly, unaccountably contented and proud of writers and the whole mysterious business of writing. So in the afternoon I cover the pages quickly, to the accompaniment of regular sharp, aggressive snores from the bow-tied members in the dimly lit writing room of a London club.

*   *   *

Another letter from a stranger. This one contains neither death threats nor requests for advice. I'm not asked to sign a book plate or help with a dissertation. What I get, on a single sheet of paper from Frankfurt, is an opening sentence which reads, 'As a man living alone, one thinks not only of one's past, but also beyond one's own being.' And he goes on, amazingly enough, 'In short, I would like to name you as my heir in my testament.'

Somewhat bewildered by this, I show the

letter to Rosie, who has an immediate reaction. 'Grab it!' Grab what, exactly? A house in Frankfurt, full of paintings of dead birds and heavy furniture? A missing Leonardo looted in the war? Something like the Maltese Falcon, which will mean that I will be shadowed by rival gangs wearing trench coats with guns weighing down their pockets?

The best legacy would be a shelf of books and a couple of candlesticks. Anyway, how old is this stranger? In the normal course of events he should be benefiting from my will, and not I from his. Too startled to come to any decision on the subject, I fold the letter up and put it away with T's description of our last hectic weekend and a bill from the Henley Garden Centre. I'll think about it later.

*   *   *

Jackie, one of the heavenly twins, has asked us to dinner, where we're to meet George Harrison. Long ago I discussed his conversion to Indian mysticism with this particular Beatle on a television show; this was at a time when I was younger, ruder and surer of my opinions. I know he lives in a stately home, complete with lodge gates and warning devices just outside Henley. We met again during a campaign to save the local cinema and he was friendly and bore me no ill will for rubbishing the once-fashionable Bhagwan. Jackie told me that

171

since the assassination of John Lennon, George lives with the constant possibility of death.

Jackie's home is also stately, sheltered by lodge gates in Shiplake, once lived in by a film star and a famous pianist. There is a bar in the corner of the billiard room, where her schoolgirl daughter is pouring out champagne. The walls are hung with the golden discs won by Deep Purple. A magnificent dinner has been arranged, starting with oysters, and a local restaurant owner is taking orders. George Harrison's son Danny is sitting, pale and shaken, in a corner. George is not there.

The night before, the Harrisons were wakened by strange noises and angry shouts. George started down the stairs, to be met by a real assassin, anxious to re-enact John Lennon's death, who attacked him with a knife. George's wife Olivia courageously beat the intruder over the head with a heavy lamp and, although he swung the light's plug at her, finally vanquished him, but not before George had been stabbed four times. Danny came home to find his parents wounded. Both George Harrison and his attacker are in hospital.

All this was going on in what used to be a sleepy and uneventful riverside town. But the horrors aren't over. Other demented people send flowers to the would-be murderer and, driving past Friar Park, raise a cheer to celebrate the attack, so deep is the hatred of success. It was an event which made no sense whatsoever, except as a tribute to a small and determined wife with a heavy lamp. Death steals up in many furtive and cowardly ways, but you don't expect to meet it coming up the stairs just because you happen to be a good musician.

CHAPTER SEVENTEEN

Conversations with a retired judge, a minor sort of judge, a circuit judge. We meet when I go into El Vino's, which is Pommeroy's wine bar in the Rumpole stories. He is sitting fondling a large whisky and gazing thoughtfully into the middle distance. His thoughts, when I have been made privy to them, have turned to sex.

'I lost my virginity to the widow of an Egyptian quantity surveyor. She was a wonderful woman, all . . . damp and that sort of thing. She taught me everything I know about the use of the elbow. It went on for years. How did you lose your virginity?'

'At a party given by a couple of lesbians, near my house in the country. I was quite young at the time. When they saw what was about to happen, they asked us to go out and do it on the common. They didn't want that

173

sort of thing to happen in their house.'

'Amazing story.' The judge is polite. 'You know my oldest son? We had a drink together in the Lamb and Flag in Croydon and he said, "I'd like you to know, Dad, I'm gay." I tell you, when he told me that, the room froze.'

'What did you say?'

'I said, "That's all right, my boy. You go on with your artistic career." Of course, I've got the other sons.'

'How old are they?'

'Seventeen and thirteen. And you know what? They've both got exceptionally large pricks.' He took a long pause for thought. 'Mine's rather small now, it comes with old age.'

He is a short, square man with bright, wary eyes that seem to be always looking for trouble, but hoping not to find it.

*   *   *

The Plinth Committee is in session and we are hearing the evidence of witnesses. Mark Wallinger is there, the artist who produced the small, vulnerable Christ, the statue which looks so lonely on the marble cube. I like Mark Wallinger, his father was a Bermondsey fishmonger and his mother went to Covent Garden almost every week to see the ballet or an opera, defying the legend that such arts are only for tired toffs and corporate entertaining.

He went to a dud art school and got a job in the now defunct communist bookshop, Colletts, on Charing Cross Road, where he spent his time reading the racing papers and placing bets. He managed to scrape up enough money to put himself through a decent art school, and started his career by painting horses. Another cast of his Christ will appear in front of the cathedral in Milan. Mark Wallinger sits quietly, waiting his turn. At the moment we are hearing the views of the late Bernie Grant, the black Labour MP for Tottenham, and his subject is slavery.

Why not a monument, a statue, a memorial on the plinth to the unknown victims of the British slave trade? Why not, indeed. The prosperity of Liverpool and Bristol was built on slavery, an easily forgotten item on our national criminal record. The wealth of the Barretts of Wimpole Street and of the family in Jane Austen's *Mansfield Park* was manured by the blood and sweat of slaves. So would not Trafalgar Square, with its triumphant celebration of the glories of Empire, be the place to remember the dark side of imperial conquest?

Bernie Grant is doing well when he suddenly expresses deep disapproval of *Ecce Homo*, which he seems to think is a national disgrace.

'So what do you think is wrong with it, exactly?' I ask Bernie.

175

'White! We find it an insult that Jesus Christ is portrayed as white.'

'He's white because that was the colour of the material I made him out of.' Mark Wallinger is prepared to come out fighting. 'I wanted a contrast to the other statues in the square, which have all gone black. At the moment we've got a black George IVth, black Generals Napier and Havelock, and a black Nelson on the top of a pillar.' It's true, all those heroes have blacked up, as in some now outlawed minstrel show.

But Bernie Grant will allow no further argument. 'It's a well-known fact,' he says, 'Jesus Christ was black and so were his disciples. They all came from Abyssinia. Anyway, it would be very appropriate to have a monument to an unknown slave in Trafalgar Square, because of the sugar ...'

'The sugar?' I am after a further explanation.

'The slaves worked on sugar plantations.'

'Yes, of course. But ...'

'And Tate and Lyle sell sugar, don't they?'

'Yes.' I have to admit it.

'And the statue would be outside the Tate Gallery.'

I feel badly about it, but I have to explain that the Tate Gallery is on the Embankment. I hope that Sainsbury's employed black slaves, because our plinth is just opposite the Sainsbury wing of the National Gallery.

All the same a reminder of the slave trade is a valuable suggestion, although Mark Wallinger is now looking at the MP for Tottenham as though the small figure on the plinth had never said that bit about forgiving your enemies.

*   *   *

I'm having another drink in El Vino's with the retired circuit judge (circus judges, Rumpole calls them), because I have become fond of him and his dialogue. With him is David, his usually silent friend. The judge is, he tells me, a devout Catholic, and spends a lot of time at what I understand to be a monastery in Croydon.

'So I got divorced,' the judge is saying, 'and I wanted to marry this really lovely lady. I went to the Cardinal. I saw Basil Hume and told him the situation, but he was against it. So I made a direct call to God!'

'How did you put it?'

'I said, "Look here, God. I've met this really lovely lady and it's my chance of a lifetime. I mean, I know I'll burn in hell if I marry her, but I'm prepared to take a chance. What do you say?"'

'And what did God say?'

'He said, "It's entirely up to you."'

This morning I got a letter and recognized T's handwriting on the envelope. Inside was a single sheet of notepaper on which were only two words. 'Arriving Tuesday.' Tuesday, then. Perhaps I'm better off with my imaginary weekends, with no danger of hell.

*   *   *

Now I know about old age. I have just set fire to a pair of trousers and a short-wave radio, a device capable of getting the BBC World Service when we're in Italy or Morocco.

I believe bonfires are now politically incorrect and it's the custom to sort your rubbish into classified bins, the bottles going in one direction and the old newspapers packed off in another, for recycling during the inevitably short period when paper will still be in demand. This clinical approach to rubbish is held by those unused to the smell of burning leaves in autumn, or who have never watched a pile of cardboard boxes flare up and collapse as satisfactorily as the skyscraper in *The Towering Inferno*, or heard the crackling of twigs on the Fifth of November, or lit driftwood on the sand for the purpose of boiling newly caught shrimps. There used to be an unpleasant judge down the Old Bailey who suggested that arsonists, when the flames shoot up as a result of their crimes, experience orgasms. Bonfires have never done this for me, but, in a purely Platonic way, I do love them. My first job is to strip down the newspapers,

178

extricating all sections dealing with business, sports, style, money matters or the internet. Focusing interest on the arts pages and the perpetual comedy of political life means that you have plenty of kindling. The supplements go first, but tomorrow the whole paper—the day's scandals, recipes and the thoughts of a dozen columnists about sex, cellulite and paternity leave—will take the primrose path to the everlasting bonfire on the blackened earth under the trees at the top of the kitchen garden. This place, where high-shooting flames make the leaves on the trees crackle and a plume of smoke spreads the news across the cabbages, will be miraculously fertile when the fire moves on. If this is hell, no wonder Don Giovanni chose it rather than the weakness of repentance and the cold comfort of purgatory.

One of my earliest memories is of a bungalow my parents rented at some seaside where, each morning, my father would run a Union Jack up an improvised flagpole and we would ceremoniously burn the contents of the waste-paper baskets and bury the leavings of the sink to the accompaniment of a song which went, 'You're the cream in my coffee, You're the sole of my shoe,' scratchily played on a wind-up gramophone. At least I learned a respect for rubbish.

About the short-wave radio. Sometimes I keep it on my pillow all night so that I can wake up from time to time to hear news of riots and elections, storms and insurrections in remote parts of the world, and receive reports from Nairobi and Singapore. In the morning I transport some of my clothes, including a pair of trousers, in an empty black plastic bag which happens to be present: I put the radio in as well, for easy carrying. In the kitchen I fill plastic bags with unwanted bits of today's, and the whole of yesterday's newspapers. Carrying full bags, I hobble, with a reasonable anticipation of delight, towards the burning area. There I find empty boxes from the Majestic Wine Warehouse, hedge clippings, branches off a spreading fig tree and the top of a broken chair. I gently apply a match to a corner of the travel section. Flames are dancing in a shaft of sunlight and, for a moment, I hear a strange, eerie sound from the centre of a melting plastic bag: it's 'Jealousy', being played, no doubt, at the request of a student from the Turks and Caicos Islands. The music dies in the spreading conflagration. Much later I discover a zip fastener, a few trouser buttons and a melted radio in the powdered grey ashes. This is the sort of thing that happens when you grow old.

*　　　*　　　*

The statue on the plinth has changed. *Behold*

180

the Man can be beheld no longer. The defenceless Jesus has gone; now we have a weighty work by Bill Woodrow. On a man's huge head rests a book, the lessons of history shut up and disregarded. Over both grows a tall tree, its roots spreading across the plinth, its branches rising towards Nelson and the sky. This is the second of Prue Leith's temporary occupants and, although plinth experts feel it won't be as popular as Wallinger's Christ, it looks imposing as men in hard hats rise up on a moving platform to unwrap it. A Minister in the Arts Department makes a speech and, as the crowd melts away, a slight and chirpy Welshwoman with red hair and glasses appears to help me walk through the traffic to the National Gallery's Sainsbury Wing, where there is a celebration party and the promise of champagne.

I'm lucky in my companion. The distance to the Sainsbury Wing can't be more than 300 yards, but the journey is long enough for me to get a glimpse of her life. She is working on a history of the Square, about which she is marvellously well informed. Two or three years ago, she was in a pub in Tottenham Court Road when she spotted a handsome Nigerian. Happily, she had absorbed enough alcohol to go up to him with a single question, 'Your place or mine?' They have lived together happily ever since and have a little boy old enough to go to a day nursery. As we go through the glass doors of the Gallery, I ask her the name of her lover.

'Nelson.' The name makes her laugh. 'Odd, isn't it? I'm studying Nelson's column by day as well as by night.'

Grateful for this confidence, I part reluctantly from my guide and go in to the collection of portraits of Christ, which starts with *The Light of the World*. Someone wrote that the Pre-Raphaelites were obsessed with beautiful young people, and that Christ holding a lantern and knocking at a door overgrown with brambles looks like a 'healthy Kiwi backpacker'.

Christ was more fortunate than Mohammed in that his religion doesn't forbid any depiction of God. But the images of the human being who brought, on any showing, the hope of justice and promise of joy to the poor and dispossessed are almost all, with the exception of Holman Hunt's back packer, of a man tormented by pain or facing terrible suffering. He is sitting on his mother's lap, receiving gifts from kings, in the fifteenth-century Italian painting attributed to Benedetto Bonfigli, but in the background he can see himself as a young man nailed to a cross. The greatest painting, in my view, Velásquez's *Christ after the Flagellation, Contemplated by the Christian Soul*, shows a young Spanish Jesus with a bullfighter's glamorous looks, still roped to a wall, exhausted by a terrible whipping, watched with pity by an angel and a child. Carrying his heavy cross, or delicately touching the neat wound in his chest, he is the young God of suffering. Perhaps it is a lesson for all the hangers and floggers, the crackers-down and the lovers of long sentences, that the God of Western Civilization chose to play the part of a man found guilty of crime and sentenced to death as a cruel and unusual punishment.

There's no denying the flaring genius of Titian and Velásquez, but I found the most moving painting at the end of the exhibition. Painted by the eccentric who led a scarcely monogamous life in a village on the Thames not far from my home, Stanley Spencer's *Resurrection* has the awkward, shy but resolute inhabitants of Cookham climbing out of their graves in the sure hope of eternity. Beside it there is a photograph of Mark Wallinger's solitary figure on the Trafalgar Square plinth proving that, even in the days of psychics and the internet, multi-faith theology, crystal gazing and lives lived according to I Ching, the image of Christ can still, although whirled around by buses and pigeons, draw all eyes to it.

CHAPTER EIGHTEEN

Bill, my father-in-law, is a year older than I am; but he has acquired a new life. Since the death of Penny's mother, he has renewed his friendship with Brenda, long ago the boss's secretary at the animal foodstuffs firm where he worked as a traveller, before he married Penny's mother and set up as an expert and successful pig farmer in the days when there were still such things as successful pig farmers. Brenda has, he is pleased to say, a nice pair of legs, and is, by half a dozen years, his junior. For her sake, he has taken to wearing a blazer with brass buttons and a silk cravat. He has also grown a grey cavalry moustache and he twiddles the ends of it proudly.

Unlike me, Bill had a heroic war, lying about his age and, as a young lieutenant, fighting the Japanese. He was commended for bravely 'holding a position although heavily outnumbered, and finding his way back to Headquarters through enemy territory'. In his wallet he carries a fragment of a hand grenade with which he was wounded in the mouth and which, after a long stay, reappeared when he had a tooth removed many years after the war. The record he has attached to this memento is

WENT INTO TOP LIP MARCH 1944 IN BURMA CAMPAIGN. CAME OUT MAY 1966 AT DENTIST IN WHITSTABLE.

Brenda has a birthday party in a hotel on the river at Runnymede. It's a great occasion with dancing, an ambulant conjuror doing startling things with a pack of cards, grandchildren taking furtive gulps of champagne and Bill giving a modestly triumphant twirl to his moustache.

As we drive away along the river, I look at the island where King John was forced to sign the Magna Carta and provide, during the following centuries, for judgement by your peers. I look at the island with particular regret because Jack Straw, the same Jack Straw Barbara urged me to have a go at, has just announced a Bill to curtail trial by jury in a huge number of what he apparently regards as unimportant cases. So forget that a great English judge, Lord Devlin, said that trial by jury is 'the light that shows the lamp of freedom burns'. Ignore William Blackstone, fellow of All Souls, Professor of Law at Oxford, who wrote in his *Commentaries* (published in 1750, it has been taken as a legal Bible both in England and America) that delays and inconveniences in the administration of the law are the price we all must pay for justice. And that 'these inroads upon this sacred bulwark of the nation [trial by jury] are fundamentally opposite to the spirit of our constitution, and that, though begun in trifles, the precedent may gradually increase in spirit, to the utter disuse of juries in cases of the most momentous concern'. Apparently not of momentous concern to the Home Office are thefts, drug offences and assaults; thousands of defendants a year accused of these crimes are to be deprived of their time-honoured, constitutional rights.

The eccentric cleric accused of stealing books, the sports star accused of assault, the police inspector accused of a drug offence—all characters whose careers and subsequent lives might be ruined by a conviction—are to be left in the hands of overworked, world-weary and often prosecution-minded stipendiary magistrates or local worthies, who rely for legal direction on their clerks. Their trials, of huge importance to them, will have to take their turn with careless drivers, drunks and kerb-crawlers, and may, as happens to many long trials in Magistrates' Courts, be heard in bits and pieces, subject to long adjournments. Such trials only give satisfaction to civil servants and politicians who can't, when it comes to the administration of the legal system, see further than the end of a five-pound note. It is very strange to me that we have a Labour Government intent on selling off Magna Carta in job lots.

Is trial by jury nothing but an old-fashioned

luxury? I remember an usher, clearing out a jury-box after a long criminal trial, who found a note from the foreman of the jury to his colleagues. It read: 'Do we all agree: 1. That the judge is a complete bastard. 2. That the judge wants this man convicted. 3. That we therefore acquit?' This approach may be shocking to civil servants and anathema to politicians, who haven't appeared for the defence in a criminal trial. They have never been up against a judge who can't resist weighing in as an extra counsel for the prosecution. Such judges may be rare nowadays, but they still exist. They put down the defence, in their summings-up, with a weary cynicism and recite the mantra: 'Of course, members of the jury, it's a matter for you. But can you really believe it . . .' One Australian judge was known to hold his nose and pull an imaginary lavatory chain after having repeated the defence evidence.

The constitutional principle which we hold dear is not to have guilt or innocence decided by experts, by officials, whether fair-minded or not, paid by the state. We were born into a society where we are all innocent until twelve ordinary citizens come back into court and pronounce us guilty. Although a criminal conviction may be more serious for some defendants than others, it is quite wrong to confine jury trials to headline-grabbing movie stars or wayward clerics. If they deserve trial

187

by jury, we all do. And just as people from ethnic minorities want to see those of their own race in the jury-box, we're all entitled to put our fate in the hands of people like us and not be left to the mercy of lawyers.

The prejudice that undoubtedly exists among politicians against juries also comes from a lack of experience of criminal trials. Decades of knocking around the Old Bailey have convinced me that, on the whole, juries take their duties extremely seriously. They listen carefully to the evidence and come to decisions, even on complicated charges, which I may not, as a defender, have liked, but which all make logical sense. It was always far easier to get a jury to see themselves in the position of participants in a violent fight in the Bricklayers' Arms, or at a dubious duel on a garage forecourt, than it was to explain contemporary life to an Old Wykehamist on the bench. And it was always a pleasure to speak to human beings whose minds were untarnished by legal precedents and who could listen to the voice of humanity.

*   *   *

It seems a long time ago, the end of the Thatcher regime and the lightning rise to power of John Major, when the 20th June Club, a collection of writers and journalists, met in Harold Pinter's and Antonia Fraser's front-room to restate left-wing values. It was a time when a good many journalists were publishing their conservative thoughts in right-wing papers. Our group attracted a good deal of well-deserved hilarity, partly because of Harold's insistence that our proceedings should be kept entirely private and our society as secret as the Freemasons, but when news of our doings got out, as it was bound to do, at least it proclaimed the support of a number of writers for the Labour Party. Among our members, who included David Hare and Salman Rushdie, was Margaret Jay, the ex-wife of an ex-Ambassador to Washington and the daughter of James Callaghan, one-time Labour Prime Minister. So we waited, eagerly, to enter the promised land of a Labour Britain, and almost lost heart when Neil Kinnock was beaten by John Major.

Then came Tony Blair, the great Labour landslide and the announcement of a paradise no longer postponed. Three years later, the promised land seems not to have changed very much from the familiar landscape in which the 20th June Club first met. However, Margaret Jay has become Labour Leader in the House of Lords, responsible for the dismissal of the majority of hereditary peers, and a member of the Cabinet. It's Sunday lunch-time and we meet in the Swan at Tetsworth, not far from our houses on the edge of the Chilterns. She is there with a number of her friends, including

189

an education minister, and in the car I was challenged by my friends Tim Cassel and Ann Mallelieu to launch a blistering attack on New Labour. I am, in fact, commendably restrained. I fail to ask whether, if a Martian were set down in Tony Blair's Britain and then transported to the land of John Major, he would notice any particular difference. I confine myself to asking what on earth the Government has got against juries.

'Nobody who lives outside the M25 cares about juries.' Lady Jay smiles, tolerant of what is clearly an eccentric concern with the principles of British justice. In fact, we both live outside London's ring road, and the Swan at Tetsworth is beyond it too.

When I point out that Jack Straw, when in opposition, had passionately opposed a Conservative plan to reduce jury trials, I am told that anyone can change their mind. Finally, both Margaret Jay and the education minister say they aren't really concerned about juries, but are more interested in problems concerning women; although women also, I suppose, might wish to get a fair trial if they were falsely accused. So I sit in a pub outside the M25, caring deeply and thinking of Runnymede, the scene of past historical events such as Brenda's birthday party and the signing of Magna Carta.

Why aren't I more grateful for a Labour Government, for which we have waited so long and hoped for so much? After the Swan at Tetsworth, I begin to wonder. Does it go back to being an only child—moreover, the only child of a blind barrister, who didn't welcome visitors because they might have felt sorry for him, and a Shavian 'new woman', a painter who buried her talent in the private garden of her marriage? For as long as I can remember, I have been able to watch myself with surprise and often disapproval, frequently finding myself ridiculous and wondering, sometimes with despair, what I might get up to next. Capable of such critical self-regard, the only child tends to be wary of outsiders and finds it difficult to feel part of any group which demands unswerving loyalty.

For this reason, I never had much interest in team games, nor did I feel particular pride in any school I happened to go to, or feel drawn to old-boy reunions. Does this explain why I've always found failure more interesting to write about than success; criminals and defence barristers more understandable than judges and prosecutors? Is it the natural position of the only child to be against the Government, whatever sort of Government it may happen to be? Lacking group loyalty, are we solitary children naturally dismissive of anyone who wants to tell us how to lead our lives?

*   *   *

191

I was sitting in the Moroccan sun when they brought me the mobile from the bar. It was Clive Conway, the flute player and manager of our gigs, and Penny heard me say 'Cleethorpes? Of course we'll do Cleethorpes!' And now, like such unavoidable occasions as birthdays and death, Cleethorpes is upon me.

We drove for three hours, up to the north-east coast where Cleethorpes and Grimsby fade into each other and where, for centuries, shoals of fish were landed from England's silver sea, and haddock and mackerel, sole and halibut slopped on to the harbour and were driven off to feed a grateful nation. Now something sad has happened. There's hardly any fishing, the fishermen have sold off their licences and the harbour has a great open space where nothing more delicious is landed than hundreds of middle-range cars which careful middle managers have bought in Europe, because that's where they're cheapest, and had shipped to England.

We performed in a huge town hall and I was back climbing dark and difficult stairs and shuffling, afraid of tripping over cables, into the light, lured by the constant need to perform.

The aged, one-legged Sarah Bernhardt, on tour and in a poor date at St Augustine, Florida, played the death scene from *Antony and Cleopatra*. A local girl called Dorothy Perott, recruited as Charmian by an advertisement in the local paper, described, to the writer Joanna Richardson, Bernhardt lying on a couch on stage with the curtain down. She had been carried there on a litter, attended by her elderly doctor. Her amputation had left nothing but a stump. She was arranged on the couch with a green rubber asp at her neck. Then the curtain rose and she spoke in her 'golden voice'. When Antony entered the scene, 'The miracle happened. For she had nothing to hold, nothing to help her, and she rose from the couch, swiftly and without seeming effort, stood erect for a moment unaided, straight and firm and strangely beautiful and then collapsed into Antony's arms. She was an old woman and she had only one leg and a stump, but she had the voice of eternity.'

No similar transformation occurs to me as I hobble on to the stage. There I drop my stick with a clatter and thud on to my seat. Then I don't move until the interval, being far less sprightly than the one-legged legend of the French theatre. Happily, the audience is lively and generous and we look smugly satisfied when we're told we've drawn the biggest house in the Grimsby and Cleethorpes Festival.

This is the second time in my life I've been to Grimsby and, on the way home, chewing a garage sandwich, I remember the first. I was in the local court defending a book called *The Seven Holes of Jade*, Jade being a Chinese girl who put herself about a bit, a work which was alleged to have a tendency to deprave and corrupt the citizens of Cleethorpes. In the end, Jade and the local bookseller were acquitted. My solicitor had left early and had asked me to drive the now liberated copies of the book back to London.

So I left with twenty copies of *The Seven Holes of Jade* in the back of an elderly Jaguar, and halfway down the motorway a nasty metallic scraping announced the fact that the exhaust had come loose. I stopped near a roadside telephone and phoned the police for help. While I was waiting, I inspected the exhaust. If I only had something to raise it up on I could detach it and go home without a length of pipe trailing along the ground. I then thought of the best possible use for my load of books, made a pile of them and detached the exhaust pipe. When this complicated piece of engineering was successfully completed, and as I had forgotten about the police and the books, I drove on. I hadn't gone far before I saw, in my mirror, an officer get out of a police car and stare, no doubt with amazed curiosity, at twenty copies of the *The Seven Holes of Jade* lying on the hard shoulder, having presumably telephoned for help.

CHAPTER NINETEEN

The room looks misty and my writing blurred. I take off my glasses, blow on them and rub them with a handkerchief. No improvement. Then I wash them in soapy water and blink through them. My eyes water and corners of the room are in impenetrable shadow. There is a darkness more alarming than that of the last good night. I think again of coming home from school and seeing my father, sitting in his dressing-gown in the bathroom while my mother squeezed toothpaste on to the brush for him. He had entered the unmentionable world of blindness.

We talked about various things, how I had got on at school, his cases in the divorce court and the state of the garden he would go on tending devotedly but would never see again. But his blindness was apparently a subject of such embarrassment to both of us that we never mentioned it. From then on he never saw me or the grandchildren that were to come.

In his time, the operation to put back detached retinas was horrific. The eye was removed for the purposes of surgery and you were forced to lie still, your head wedged between sand bags for a long period of post-operative torture. My father faced a number of these operations, all unsuccessful, with a courage he couldn't muster when faced with something he really feared and hated, like a soft-boiled egg.

About thirty years after his death, I was in the office of a television company, giving out bursaries to young and clear-sighted playwrights, when half the room was plunged into darkness and the faces to the left of me vanished into the gloom. Then, also, I was hopelessly polishing my glasses; but the next morning I was on the operating table, spared the sand bags, but with a scarred retina which made me almost completely blind in one eye.

The night I came out of the hospital, we were having dinner with Barbara Castle. When I poured the wine it went over the tablecloth. I apologized and told her I couldn't see out of one eye. 'You're bloody lucky,' she said in the down-to-earth, no-nonsense tones of Old Labour. 'I'm going blind in both of them.' It's true that she can now only read huge letters with the help of a magnifying glass. But her cheerfulness and ability to knock out an opponent with a speech are in no way diminished.

When I was seventy, I got a letter from the licensing department in Swansea telling me I had to apply for a new driving licence and asking me if I had any physical disabilities. Penny told me that I mustn't lie, so I wrote back truthfully, admitting that I couldn't see out of one eye so I was no good at pouring wine or judging distances. I also had to confess that the other eye wasn't marvellous and that I had never been very good at driving, having on one occasion driven a car into the wall of my house, which failed to take evasive action. By return of post I got a letter back from Swansea, which included a new three-year licence. It ended with the cheerful message, 'Happy Motoring!' As an act of mercy to the public at large I am, however, no longer at the wheel.

My father was in middle life, at the height of his profession, when he went blind. Perhaps at my age blindness wouldn't be so terrible. I wouldn't be able to look at pictures, but so many Manets and Matisses, Velásquezes and Piero della Francescas are photographed in my mind that it might not matter. My father left me, as well as glaucoma, enough poems and speeches from Shakespeare to keep in my head, and all the best books are on tape.

I can still imagine the garden round the house and the long borders that my father could only touch and smell. Blindness must, at least, be more bearable if you can remember the world, put faces to voices, the colours of flowers to their smell, and remember the room you walk across in the dark, your hand stretched out in case you blunder into a wall or knock against the furniture.

To be born blind must be the unimaginable,

undeserved curse of an uncaring fate. Milton, considering how his light was spent, only had to regret half his days 'in this dark world and wide', but to be born having never seen a smile, a galloping horse or a sky at dawn—how could you possibly imagine or create a world? It's as impossible to conceive a blind Dickens, who had never seen a dead body or an urban slum, as it is to think of a blind Degas. We can only have the dimmest idea of the world which is lived in by those who have never seen it.

My father was, of course, privileged. He could have his briefs read to him and fool witnesses into thinking that he could see them shifting and shuffling under his ruthless questions. I suppose I could get used to a way of writing which meant talking to a machine. But for many blind people in the world, loss of sight means loss of work, safety, sanity and survival. Being without it means poverty, neglect, early death, or being the resented and useless member of the family, led about by grumbling children when they can remember. River blindness, spread by the bite of the Simulian fly which breeds on the banks of the Niger, afflicts half the people who drink the water and wash in the river. So I clean my glasses again and, shining a strong light on the ruled paper, do my best to read my own handwriting.

*　　*　　*

My father could still see when he took us—I was then about twelve—to see *Hamlet*. We sat in the front row of the stalls in stiff evening clothes. I had just got my first dinner jacket, which I wore with a soft collar, following the example of the Prince of Wales. My father and I smelt faintly of the dry cleaner's and of mothballs, a smell qualified, in his case, by a splash of eau de cologne on the handkerchief. My mother was in a brown, lacy evening gown. As the curtain went up, I dug into the box of chocolates which was the equivalent, in the West End theatre of the thirties, of popcorn in the multi-screen cinema. And then I was in the black and brown, the autumnal Elsinore, lit by the glint on helmets and swords and the crown of Denmark.

The prince was thin, tall, nervous, handsome and ironic. I enjoyed watching him tease Polonius, telling him that old men's faces are wrinkled, their eyes purging thick amber and plum-tree gum and that they have most weak hams, a condition I never expected to attain. He may not have been a great physical actor (a critic once said that 'below the waist Mr Gielgud means absolutely nothing'), but his voice gave the poetry unforgettable music and meaning and, as he said himself, although he played other parts, he *was* Hamlet. As usual, my father, sitting next to me, joined audibly in all the soliloquies, giving the star

199

some little-needed help.

Last night it was announced that John Gielgud, after a lifetime of wonderful acting, chain-smoking, chattering, dropping bricks and enjoying gossip, had died aged ninety-six. Today the papers are full of stories about him. After a childhood when he was, for me, the voice of Shakespeare, after having been such a fan that I wrote up for a signed photograph of him wearing his sensitive, aloof smile under a trilby hat, I could hardly believe my luck when I not only met him but came to write words for him to say. He confessed that he was not greatly interested in things that didn't concern him or the theatre. There was a sort of unworldliness about the man which showed itself at our first meeting.

It was at a dinner in a director's house in London. Emily was a baby then, and we had brought her with us in a carry-cot and left her in a spare bedroom. When it was time to leave we were lugging this pink plastic box out of the front door. Gielgud looked down at it and said, in some surprise, 'Why didn't you leave your baby at home? Are you afraid of burglars?'

All the stories of Gielgud as an elegant brick-dropper have been remembered. He took some pleasure in these social gaffes which were, I'm sure, unintentional at the time of utterance. I particularly like the one involving a playwright of the thirties, improbably called

Edward Knoblock. He and John Gielgud were having lunch in The Ivy in those distant days, when a man came in at the door and waved at the actor. 'Who was that man who waved at you?' Knoblock asked. 'That's the second most boring man in London.' 'Really? And who is the first most boring man in London?' Here Gielgud's subconscious swam to the surface and he answered, without hesitation, 'Oh, Edward Knoblock, of course.' And then, realizing he had dropped another hefty brick, he tried to mend matters by adding, 'I don't mean you, of course. The *other* Edward Knoblock.'

As I grew up, the theatre was dominated by two stars. Olivier, of the clipped, icily clear diction, was the great physical actor, dropping from a great height like an avenging angel to kill Claudius, or hanging suspended by his ankles as Coriolanus dead. The other was Gielgud, the master of poetry whose voice could move an audience to tears. His own tears came easily, without effort, as a result of being a member of an old theatrical family, the Terrys, who had, he told me, 'excessive lachrymal glands'; his mother was 'constantly crying like a wet April'.

As he grew too old for the nervous prince, he became a miraculous comic actor, using the impeccable voice to utter unexpected or even, as in the film *Arthur*, obscene lines. We were in Tuscany together when he acted, to my pride and joy, the dissolute old journalist, who only goes on family holidays to irritate his nearest and dearest, in an adaptation of *Summer's Lease*, a book of mine. Well over eighty, he popped home for a short operation and then returned to Italy to work, smoke and talk without drawing breath. He played Charles Ryder's father in *Brideshead Revisited*. The scene in which he derides his son's earnest request for money—'I've never been "short", as you so painfully called it. And yet what else can you say? Hard up? Distressed? Embarrassed? Stony broke? In Queer Street? Let's say you're in Queer Street and leave it at that'—became in Gielgud's hands a masterpiece of comic acting. Like the ageing Olivier, he took most of the jobs offered him, a desperate urge to get as much work done as possible before the final exit. A generation past retirement age, he learned the entire Grand Inquisitor's speech from *The Brothers Karamazov* for a schools' television broadcast. He was often to be seen queueing outside the latest movie and was never unwelcoming, sullen or dull. His failures, he always said, taught him more than his successes. With a success, 'You get praised for the wrong things and your bad habits are encouraged. With a failure you really have to *think* about where you've gone wrong.'

A year or two ago, I was talking to Alec Guinness at a party and he told me he felt too old for acting. I pointed out that Gielgud never seemed to stop. 'Johnny always liked acting,' the solemn, sepulchrally deep Guinness voice gave its verdict. 'The rest of us often thought it was a rather silly profession.'

I don't know. Giving a twelve-year-old boy a *Hamlet* to remember for life doesn't seem silly to me.

CHAPTER TWENTY

What happened to global warming? It's April and I wake to see the garden under January snow, the pink flowers shaken off the earliest rhododendrons, the white camelias browned with cold and the full-blown daffodils broken, their flowers shrunk and puckered like old men's fingers. I have to get up and slosh through the snow about the business of a play.

The hard thing about plays is the difficulty of writing 120 pages which are going to keep an audience glued to their seats, either laughing in unison or sunk into a deep and attentive silence. I am also thinking of Jean Marais and his lover Cocteau and a summer evening in Italy three years ago when Marais, in his eighties and making a film in the Tuscan countryside, came to dinner. He was still good-looking, if not the beautiful young man of Cocteau's films *Orphée* and *La Belle et La Bête*.

He told us that everybody had someone in their life they would give everything for, but he would have given up his life for Cocteau. He also told us that one day Cocteau asked him what three things he would like best to do in a play. Jean Marais said that, in the first act, 'I'd like to be on the stage all the time but not speak. In the second, I'd like to weep tears of joy, and in the third I'd like to roll down a long staircase.' Having heard this, Cocteau wrote *The Eagle Has Two Heads*, in which his friend and lover could perform all three acts. I can only envy a writer who could put a play together so easily. On the whole, I have found it a mistake to write a play for one particular actor. He or she probably doesn't want to do it and then it really doesn't suit anyone else.

The play I've written has to do with judges. Those who undertake the business of being a High Court judge condemn themselves to what are, in many ways, terms of imprisonment. They have to travel the country, far from their homes and loved ones, and do time in strange houses set aside for the confinement of judges, until they have sat through all the trials in one city and move on to the next.

These 'safe houses' usually shelter three judges, one to deal with criminal cases, another with civil cases, and another strong enough to face the more painful and deeper horrors of family law. So these three are thrown together, and used to be forbidden to drink in pubs or go to the movies without a police escort, in case they were got at and corrupted by the local inhabitants. I became interested in the way these men and women, deciding the destinies of their fellow citizens, spend their spare time and cope with their fellows.

Eccentricity, I know, tends to break out.

One seasoned judge told me that he always travelled with a small replica of that childhood favourite, Paddington Bear. Paddington sat, hidden by books and papers, on the judge's desk when he was trying murder cases. When the butler packed for him to move to the next town, the judge asked what had happened to Paddington, and was told that the small, gumbooted bear was safely in the suitcase. 'In the suitcase? Are you mad?' The judge, always even-tempered in Court, was now seriously angry. 'Paddington will suffocate in a suitcase. He likes to sit in the car next to the driver, with the window slightly open, so he can breathe in the fresh air and admire the scenery.'

Auden wrote:

> In the burrows of the Nightmare,
> When justice naked is,
> Time watches from the shadow
> And coughs when you would kiss.

So I called my play *Naked Justice*, and it started the usual slow and accident-prone

205

progress towards a production. I have management in the shape of Duncan Weldon, who started life as a photographer and is engagingly stage-struck, with rooms full of old programmes and posters. He was once married briefly to Helen Shapiro, a pop singer of the sixties whose hit number was 'Walking Back to Happiness'. At times of stress, Duncan looks doubtful, scratches his beard and suggests the employment of various inappropriate stars who will inflate box-office takings.

I also have Leslie Phillips to play the oldest and most likeable judge. He's been an actor since he was eleven years old, a child in a Gielgud production who went on to be an Assistant Stage Manager before the war. After it, he was the star of Doctor films and numberless comedies, and matured into a remarkably funny and touching actor. For a long time he was in love with Penelope's daughter, my step-daughter Caroline, and their relationship was so happy that I had to face, with what courage I could muster, the prospect of being called Dad by Leslie Phillips. The danger passed and they are now safely married to others.

I also have a director, Christopher Morahan, whose somewhat military bearing conceals a great enthusiasm for the theatre and an admirable attention to detail. There is a hope, which may well, like other theatrical aspirations, fade, that we might start rehearsing in August.

On this sunny morning, I'm off to see another impresario, Don Taffner, who has greatly enriched the lives of British writers by selling our work to American television. He has elegant offices in New York, Sydney and Bedford Square, two of which I have officially opened as She Who Must Be Obeyed's buildings, with a blue plaque on the front wall honouring Don's wife, Eleanor. Eleanor is a gifted shopper who has acquired a taste for the art nouveau furniture of Charles Rennie Mackintosh, and the Taffners have bought a Mackintosh house in Glasgow. So now I am going to the Eleanor Taffner building in London, because Don has read the play about the judges and wants to take part in the production.

He is a small, enormously energetic man with poor eyesight, who began life as an office boy in a firm doing publicity for Broadway theatres. He laughs a lot and still seems to enjoy his business hugely. It took no time for him to discuss his participation in the production and the help he could give us, and then his thoughts turned, I thought unexpectedly, to Napoleon's dick.

I had heard that Duncan was mounting an ambitious musical about the Emperor at Don's theatre, the Shaftesbury. When we discuss this, Don's voice becomes dreamy and he says he has a catalogue which lists the unknown treasures in the world's small museums. To his surprise, he discovered a museum in New York in which, pickled I suppose, reposes a vital part of Napoleon, sold off with other bits and pieces by the doctor who undertook his post-mortem. The plan is to bring it over and exhibit it in the foyer at the opening of Duncan's musical. A suggestion of activating it electronically during a love duet is not to be taken seriously. When Don's secretary asks for a description of this historic remnant, it is said to be 'long and leathery'. Later I discover that this trophy was once put up for sale by a great auction house, but, at the insistence of the French Government, it was withdrawn.

For an ultimate destination it's hard to decide between burial and cremation. I can't feel that many men would like to have their pickled penises displayed at the opening of a musical; but perhaps that's what the army he deserted in the snows of Russia would have wanted for Bonaparte.

*   *   *

Today, Mr Roy Burnett, aged fifty-seven, was released after serving fourteen years of a life sentence for rape. In 1986, at the Old Bailey, a young student nurse said, in evidence, that Mr Burnett, then a gardener, had attacked her, pulled her down into some bushes, raped her

208

and committed another sexual assault. In 1998, the same woman made an undoubtedly false allegation of rape to the Devon police. This led to a hearing in the Court of Appeal, where it was revealed there was no evidence of blood or semen in the original trial, and the woman in question now refused to come to Court to repeat her evidence. There were so many inconsistencies in her case that the Appeal Court judge came to the conclusion that the allegations of rape and assault were not true. Mr Burnett has lost fourteen years of his life because of an event 'which almost certainly never happened'. One of the most alarming aspects of the case is that he was consistently refused parole because he steadfastly maintained his innocence.

I had, egged on by Barbara Castle, chided the Home Secretary, Jack Straw, for rashly assuming the guilt of men accused of rape and refusing them full rights of cross-examination and the ability to conduct their own defence. Two days before the Appeal judgement in Mr Burnett's case, the Home Office received a report Jack Straw had ordered from a 'working party of civil servants', which simply and outrageously suggested that in rape cases, the burden of proving consent should shift from the Prosecutor to the Accused. My learned friend Horace Rumpole, known to many as Rumpole of the Bailey, has one great article of faith. He believes, above all things, in what has been rightly called the golden thread that runs through British justice—the presumption of innocence. If any one of us is accused of a crime, we are innocent and remain so until at least ten of our fellow citizens are sure, beyond reasonable doubt, that we must be guilty. This, our great safeguard against the conviction of the innocent, is what makes our system safer than continental trials, in which the accused starts off as a suspect and is found guilty by judicial inquiry. But for the authors of this report, the golden thread is no more than a worn-out bit of binder twine which can, in the new age of political correctness, be thrown away like other old-fashioned articles such as trial by jury.

How, for instance, is a man who has had sex, perhaps after a date, to prove consent beyond reasonable doubt? There are unlikely to be witnesses. Will he be acquitted only if his partner told the waiter, the taxi driver and the party of neighbours downstairs that she was simply longing to go to bed with him? If, as is most likely, it's only her word against his, it would be monstrous if the case were to be decided by a presumption of guilt. What it would mean is that defendants would sit in prison, and perhaps get life sentences, not because the jury was sure of guilt, but because they might have some reservations about the defence. Penal sentences would no longer depend on certainty, but on doubt.

What is sad is the feeling of having waited so long for a powerful Labour Government, which would improve social justice, care for public services, nurture the Arts and protect civil liberties, only to get one whose ideas of justice can be dictated by focus groups and last week's headlines, and not by tried and respected principles. Today, there's a great deal of talk about Englishness and the things we have to be proud of. High on the list of such valued national possessions, as Rumpole says, are the plays of Shakespeare, the herbaceous border, the presumption of innocence and the great British breakfast. Of these, the presumption of innocence may be said to share first place with the plays of Shakespeare. The report by Home Office boffins should, as soon as possible, be consigned to the nearest dustbin.

*　　　*　　　*

The snow melted, there's even sunshine and the smell of grass drying. I'm getting dressed to go to London again for further business about the play. My father shouted for company as he stood, feeling for the tie or the waistcoat set out, hanging on to the end of his bed, complaining loudly of the loneliness of getting dressed. Byron regretted the huge part of our lives spent buttoning and unbuttoning. Old men should, many of them do, dress in the fashion of their prime. After seventy, it's probably wise to avoid a long grey ponytail, or allow the body, to sag and the neck to be exhibited in a beige unstructured suit and a white T-shirt. Costume drama on television makes the mistake of dressing all its men in the same period; the old do their best to look as they did forty years ago. So I'm climbing into a fully structured suit with a waistcoat, dealing with cufflinks and a tie, strenuously avoiding any sort of ponytail. And yet, at lunch-time, I am to discover it's not always wise to cling to the dress code of the past.

I have come up to London to meet Sally Green, a remarkably beautiful theatre owner and play-angel, who lets drop the fact that when she was very young she met Frank Sinatra, with whom she agreed to have an assignation. All went well until, as she jumped on to the bed, he appeared from the bathroom wearing what she described as 'long knickers and braces on his socks'. It was the braces, she said, that did it. She burst into uncontrollable laughter, he got angry and the romance froze in the cold waters of mockery and offence. I suppose the lesson of this is that unless you have entirely abandoned hope, and however fashionable they were when you were young, give up the sock suspenders.

CHAPTER TWENTY-ONE

I that in heill was and gladnèss
Am trublit now with great sickness
And feblit with infirmitie:
Timor Mortis conturbat me.

The man troubled by the fear of death was William Dunbar, Scottish poet, believed to have been born in or around 1460, probably in East Lothian, although the date and circumstances of his birth and death remain shrouded in mystery. It's certain that he joined the Franciscans and admitted that he found himself wholly unfitted for the life of a begging friar. In fact, he used his period of monkhood to sow his wild oats and it was said that 'wrinkle, wile and falsehood filled his days so long as he did beir the friar's style'. In the habit of his order, he confessed he made good cheer in every flourishing town in England between Berwick and Calais. He seems to have come over the wall without difficulty and became a salaried poet at the court of James IV of Scotland. After the battle of Flodden, there is little record of his existence. He wrote a good deal of satirical poetry, including 'The Dance of the Sevin Deidly Synnis'. He battled in verse with his friend Kennedy, each poet aiming wounding insults at the other. He also wrote a poem with the irresistible title 'The Twa Maryit Wemen and the Wedo'. From all we know of him he had an eventful and enjoyable life and no doubt relished his irrepressible talent. But he was troubled by the fear of death. Dunbar was especially worried by the fact that death seemed to have it in for writers.

> 'He has done petuously devour
> The noble Chaucer'

There then followed a whole list of writers wiped out by this common complaint.

> 'That scorpion fell has done infeck
> Maister John Clerk, and James Afflek,
> Fra ballat-making and tragedie:—
> *Timor Mortis conturbat me . . .*
>
> He has reft Mersei his endite,
> That did in luve so lively write,
> So short, so quick, of sentence hie:—
> *Timor Mortis conturbat me.*
>
> He has tane Rowll of Aberdene,
> And gentill Rowll of Corstorphine;
> Two better fallowis did no man see:—
> *Timor Mortis conturbat me.*

I'd become haunted by this poem, but when I found it in Helen Gardner's *The New Oxford*

Book of English Verse, I discovered that she had cut out the names of the dead writers, except for Chaucer, the Monk of Bury and Gower, and replaced them with a neat asterisk. To recall the others, I had to go back to Rumpole's preferred Sir Arthur Quiller-Couch edition, *The Oxford Book of English Verse*. So Mersei, 'that did in luve so lively write', and the two good fellows named Rowll were not only wiped out by death but consigned to oblivion by Helen Gardner. Now there is good news of a resurrection. Professor Christopher Ricks, in a third edition, has recalled them all from the grave, so the two Rowlls can live on, together with Blind Harry, Sandy Traill and Patrik Johnstoun.

There is a line of poets from Keats to Sylvia Plath who seem to have found something sexy and alluring, some quality to fall in love with in death. Germaine Greer has said that Plath's poetic death-wish has had the undesirable effect of tempting young girls to top themselves. She thinks they'd be better off reading some cheerful masterpiece such as Byron's *Don Juan*, a verdict with which I entirely concur.

For me Dunbar, the good-time monk, got it right when he thought of death not as a mysterious love object but as a vague, unexplained anxiety. *Timor mortis*, like arthritis and failing eyesight, sets in around seventy and becomes acute after seventy-five.

There are, however, if not cures, at least painkillers, placebos and periods of remission.

Love, the opening of a bottle of champagne or the act of writing sentences to fill a long sheet of ruled paper can banish *timor* at least temporarily. The cure is to be found among the living, not dwelling with those good fellows, Rowll of Aberdeen and Rowll of Corstorphine, reduced to an asterisk by death and the editor of an anthology.

* * *

My birthday. Strangely enough, *timor mortis*, from which I have been suffering from time to time, has diminished, probably because at this age it's really no use worrying. Penny gives me a signet ring with a dormouse's head on it, and then goes off, with a party of friends, bonefishing from an oil rig five hours away from the coast of Cuba. I was invited to join them, and toyed with the idea until it became clear that the only way to my bedroom would be up a rope ladder. I don't want to be a party pooper, but the idea of going to bed, with two ineffective knees and a stick, up a rope ladder on an oil rig five hours off the coast of Cuba seems, strangely enough, unattractive.

So I stay at home and take Rosie out to dinner. She's about to be sixteen, and has been staying with the family of an eighteen-year-old boy, who is in love with her. Before Christmas, she told me, she was on the point of giving him the push because he was 'too nice to me when I was ill'.

I suppose I know what she means, but even so, life has become pretty tough for young men. You've got to seem aloof, but how do you judge the moment when uncaring, even bad behaviour ceases to be challenging and attractive and you're merely another pain in the neck. Men, of course, as the weaker sex, make no such obscure demands. When they get a touch of flu, all they require is constant, wholehearted and anxious attention.

For my birthday, Rosie gave me some CDs. Her choice echoes my past, Van Morrison as well as 'American Pie' and *The Greatest Hits of the Everley Brothers*. I suppose our pop tunes are the music we fell in love to, which in my case stretches from 'You are my Sunshine' and 'There'll Be Blue Birds Over the White Cliffs of Dover' to Elvis and Tommy Steele, the Beatles and the Rolling Stones, through to the strange songs Penny and I danced to when we first met, which had such embarrassing refrains as 'Yummy, yummy, yummy, I got love in my tummy'. We also had, when we started life together, a Bob Dylan album—almost our only article of furniture. After a childhood devoted to Fred Astaire and Ginger Rogers, playing a one-man band to accompany Radio Luxembourg, I grew up to think the words the most important ingredient of any song.

217

I've discovered few contemporary lyrics to admire, although I became a great fan of one about wanting to 'sleep with the common people' by Jarvis Cocker of Pulp. In a moment of total madness I elected to try to sing it to a karaoke machine at a party. The result was ghastly and as embarrassing as Frank Sinatra's sock suspenders. Perhaps the old should stick to the music of their prime.

On the way out of the restaurant, I called at the Gents and found Dickie Attenborough, who regretted that our Old Testament stories had never reached the television screens of America. 'This man on the network,' he told me, 'said, "We've got two Madonnas and a Mary Magdalene and a couple of Jesuses in the can, so we just haven't got room for any more Bible."'

*   *   *

A week later and Penny is back, full of traveller's tales, accounts of swimming among barracudas, fishing in mosquito-infested swamps, and the test for scuba divers which entailed diving to thirty metres, catching a bonefish and kissing a shark, all on the same day. All things considered, I feel I was wise to stay at home. One of her stories, however, contains an unforgettable image, surpassing anything yet dreamed of by Damien Hurst.

Cuba, it seems, has an excellent education

system, low infant mortality, period motor cars and laws against any sort of private enterprise or trading, which means that all cattle have to be handed over to the government when ready for slaughter. The result of this law is that Cubans have become expert at killing and butchering in five minutes flat and that the police constantly search cars for carefully packed, illicit Sunday dinners.

Castro thought it would be interesting and productive to introduce water buffalo to the island. These animals, in hot weather, were accustomed to stand up to their necks in swamps in order to keep cool. Platoons of police kept watch over them and made a careful head count. In time, the officers noticed that many of the heads had started to droop and their eyes looked distinctly exhausted. Further investigation into the swamp revealed that about a hundred of the bodies had been carved into saleable joints and nothing remained but a herd of heads on poles, to symbolize the collapse of communist economics.

CHAPTER TWENTY-TWO

An invitation to a dinner of legal executives. In the days when I knocked about the Probate, Divorce and Admiralty Division, they were known as 'managing clerks', and had no legal qualifications except common sense, a lifetime's experience and a deeper knowledge of the mysterious process of issuing writs and filing documents than the solicitors who employed them. They came in two varieties, either fat and cheerful, their pockets stuffed with summonses and affidavits, who would pant up the steps of the Law Courts and take a cheerfully optimistic view of your chances, 'You'll pull it off, sir. You can see further through a brick wall than him they've briefed agin us.' Or thin, and gloomily ironic. 'Do what you can for her, sir, in my view, our woman doesn't deserve a penny.' During the long wait outside court, it was important to get on well with the managing clerks and ask them pertinent questions about their chrysanthemums or their daughter's ballroom dancing, so that they would remember you and call round with highly paid briefs in their overcoat pockets. Even the most pessimistic would exhibit some signs of cheerfulness when the briefs were in Probate Actions, for wills always produced bitter and ruthlessly contested litigation, the huge costs of which would be paid by the dead.

The will seemed, for old people, the last gasp of power, the final chance to make mischief and sow some dissension from beyond the grave. If the soul is immortal, I wonder if it enjoys gazing down on courtrooms full of brothers and sisters, uncles and aunts, wives and lovers, who have come to hate each other in the struggle for pieces of furniture, bungalows in Sussex, small annuities or a lifetime's savings which have no value in eternity. These were the cases lawyers dreamt of and I remember one which lasted, to our great satisfaction, for a year in court; a proceeding so precious and expensive that the parties insured the life of the judge. The deceased owned a German telephone company and he had scattered at least eight wills, variously benefiting the main characters in his life: his mother, his wife, his chauffeur and a number of mistresses, including a Jamaican lady diplomat and a mysterious beauty who had been reduced to living in an abandoned car on the Via Veneto in Rome, while she waited for her inheritance. There was also the dead man's psychiatrist, who seemed to have been left a great deal of money in some of the wills and to whom the other beneficiaries, divided about everything else, were united in enmity. On one occasion, as he lay in bed in some German castle, the unhappy testator was surrounded by his mother, his chauffeur and his psychiatrist, all interested in different wills.

As this case wound its slow progress through the Probate Court, the barrister sitting next to me, against whom I'd been fighting, pulled out a document from the pile in front of him and asked me to sign at the 'foot or end thereof.' Nobody learns from experience; he was asking me to witness his will.

*   *   *

The divorce court provided a slightly rosier view of human nature and surprising insights into family life behind the net curtains in Wimbledon and Hampstead Garden Suburb. When I started, it was a strange period in the matrimonial law of England; you could get a decree ordering your spouse to restore your 'conjugal rights', and a husband could sue his wife's lover for damages. Such cases provided a problem for the Co-respondent. He had to show that he had seduced a second-rate wife, a rotten cook and careless mother, hardly worth more than a tenner by way of compensation. It was a sad ending to adulterous passion. In these days of 'no-fault' divorce decrees, the procedure that ends a marriage seems to amount to not much more than filling in a form before saying 'Cheerio.' When I started, you had to prove something terribly serious, like adultery. One of my first clients was a husband who was finding it enormously difficult to persuade anyone to commit adultery with his wife. He was reduced to the terrible expedient of putting on a false beard, a false moustache and a pair of dark glasses and creeping into his own bungalow acting, for the benefit of the neighbours, the part of his own Co-respondent.

The sad result was that he was sent to prison for 'perverting the course of justice'. I thought that was more than a little hard. After all, if you can't sleep with your own wife wearing a false beard, what can you do?

What the young barrister learns is that it's possible to bear other people's troubles with great fortitude and solve other people's problems with no trouble at all. He'll no doubt leave his home in the morning after a terrible row with his wife, bleeding at the nostril and with his shirt torn. He'll stagger down the stairs. The *au pair* girl will be pregnant and have left home, the children suffering from infectious diseases. He'll yank the front door open against a mound of bills, the overdraft will have been frozen and the mortgage foreclosed. Out in the street he'll find his car has been stolen, and he'll thumb a lift to his chambers in the Temple. Once there, he'll be perfectly capable of advising a sixty-year-old property developer on exactly how he should conduct his married life.

The form-filling end to marriage has denied us wonderful insights into what politicians say they revere as 'family life'. I remember appearing in a divorce case in which the following unforgettable scene was central. The vicar's wife and the (female) district nurse were locked in a passionate embrace in the matrimonial bedroom, behind a locked door which the vicar (unfortunately my client) was trying to break down with the spade used by the sexton for the digging of graves.

The conclusion to this everyday story of country folk was that the vicar and I lost, but we argued for the custody of the children on the basis that they needed the influence of a man in their lives. This plea failed when the judge was told that the district nurse had changed her sex and was now fully prepared to be that man.

It wasn't all as colourful as this. Most clients were decent enough men and women who'd just married the wrong person. What was remarkable was not the light-hearted way they parted, but the dogged persistence with which they would put up with disloyalty, prolonged silences and wearying contempt. They did have a good deal of simple faith in marriage, provided it was to a different wife or husband. What was sad was that so many seemed to go through the painful and expensive business of divorce in order to marry someone who bore a marked similarity to the spouse they had just dismissed, but was a bit drunker, meaner and less attractive.

I am talking to an old barrister, long ago retired, like me, and we are remembering the great days of reading sensational divorce cases. We recollect the facts of the Russell case. Lady

Russell, it was agreed on all sides, was a virgin when she gave birth. How did this miraculous event occur? 'She had sat on the laps of Guards Officers in Skindles Hotel, Maidenhead,' said Lord Russell.

Not at all, his wife countered. It had all happened because she made unsuitable use of 'His Lordship's sponge', which he had left around the bathroom with sperm, presumably, nestling in it. This case caused such embarrassment to the House of Lords that they passed the rule in the Russell case which, for a long while, made it illegal for one party in a marriage to give evidence of non access to the other which might tend to render their children illegitimate.

That was all very interesting, says my old barrister friend, but just consider the evidence of these two consecutive witnesses in another famous and aristocratic divorce, in which the wife was alleged to have taken many Polaroid snaps during her various infidelities. Several hundreds of these photographs were put in evidence at the trial. The part of the proceedings my learned and retired friend is referring to went something like this:

Counsel: (*to the first witness*): Are you Mr Blank, a jeweller of Bond Street?

Witness: I am.

Counsel: Will you take in your hand Exhibit 89. Have you got it?

Witness: Yes, I have.

Counsel: Is that a picture of a hand holding a penis?

Witness: So it would seem.

Counsel: Ignore the penis. Concentrate on the hand. What can you tell us about the ring on the third finger?

Witness: That is the diamond and ruby item I set in a gold ring for her ladyship.

Counsel: Thank you.

There were no questions from the other side.

Counsel: I will now call Dr Blank of Harley Street. Dr Blank, will you now take in your hand Exhibit Number 89. Have you got it?

Witness: Yes, I have.

Counsel: Is that a picture of a hand holding a penis?

Witness: So it would seem.

Counsel: Ignore the hand. What can you tell us about the penis?

Witness (without hesitation): *Not* His Lordship's.

The prolonged litigation connected with the Russell case led to a contest about the descent of the peerage and the identity of the rightful heir. This case was won by the present Lord Ampthill, whose mother had gone through an unusual birth process. Geoffrey Ampthill is a popular peer, elected to remain in the House of Lords after its decimation by New Labour. He turned up at the Gazelle d'Or Hotel in Morocco, full of charm and bubbling with energy at seventy-eight.

Although he said he 'only really liked talking to birds', he did announce that when he was a baby he had, at the old trial, 'been passed round the jury three times and then taken by his mother on a seven-day journey across the Atlas mountains on muleback through the snow'. That seems to me to be a babyhood to be proud of.

CHAPTER TWENTY-THREE

Well! Would you believe it? Is it coffee, lunch, tea, dinner, bednight or all three? If you haven't appeared by 5.30 p.m. I shan't know whether to go to Evensong or not. I'm not sure I'm all that keen to go to Evensong anyway, as Priscilla's manifestations are very offputting.
                    Optimistically, T.

I'm rather glad to hear from T. Unlike real love letters, they threaten no blame, guilt or remorse and call for no elaborate planning or devious plots, no righteous self-denial. The thought of coffee and bednight poses no threats, and Priscilla's manifestations at Evensong are a matter of perpetual interest. I fold the letter neatly, and put it away with gratitude.

                    *   *   *

I have a drink with David, the ex-judge's friend. He's in a sad, elegiac mood. I buy him a glass of red wine and he tells me, 'I've had some knocks in my life and now my wife has given me the elbow.'
    'Good heavens. How did that happen?'
    'Well, we were watching one of those

television drama things and at the end it said, "starring" somebody and "featuring" somebody else. So I asked Christine, that's my wife, you know. I said, "Christine! What's the difference between 'starring' and 'featuring'?"'

'What did she say?'

'She said, "Take our marriage, for instance. Our marriage is 'starring Christine' and 'featuring David'." I suppose it was true in a way, but after that she bunked off.'

*   *   *

Mr Halmi, the Head of Hallmark Entertainment and producer of exotic, spectacular and star-studded films of the great stories, myths and legends of many lands, has just acquired a network which will show his films for twenty-four hours a day, with hardly a break for coffee, the loo, love-making or the news, from Shanghai to Bombay, from the shopping malls of Basingstoke to the condos of California. To celebrate this global acquisition, he gives a banquet in the ballroom of Claridge's, where the doorway is lit by flaming torches.

I sit next to Mr Halmi at a round table which also seats Peter Barnes, an excellent playwright, and Christopher Lee, better known as Count Dracula. As we talk, the figures, as essential to a banquet as waiters, of the conjuror, the silhouette maker and the drawer

229

of caricatures, wander silently round us.

'Hungary,' Mr Halmi tells me. 'I was born in Hungary and my father was Court photographer to the last of the Hapsburgs.' Then came the complete history of mid-European politics from Admiral Horthy to the war, from the Communists to the Germans and the Russians, from wealth and success to gaol.

'I was finally,' Mr Halmi said, as a conjuror in a maroon turban lit a fifty-pound note and recovered it from Count Dracula's ear, 'condemned to be hanged.'

Around us, innumerable television sets were alive with burning ships, charging horses, exotic Cleopatras, angry wizards, mad March hares and pint-sized Lilliputians. Mr Halmi had been sprung from gaol and was on a boat to America with no more than five dollars in his pocket. Arriving on Ellis Island, he was given a blood test, his chest was cursorily examined and he was let into the country. It wasn't long before he became a photographer with Time Life and, eventually, the owner of a worldwide television network.

I wonder how many potential Halmis are being turned away from England as 'bogus asylum seekers'.

Peter Barnes admits he always writes film scripts in a burger bar near Shaftesbury Avenue, to the accompaniment of loud piped music and the sizzling of fries. If he has to write a play, he retires to the privacy of his office.

After all this information, and a few glasses of champagne, I make the long journey to the Claridge's Gents. An Italian in white gloves is in charge of filling the washbasin and brushing dandruff off the guests' collars. He greets me with a glad cry of, 'I see you at the Opera in San Gimignano! *Rigoletto*!' We sing together, hopelessly out of tune, 'La Donna È Mobile' whilst he fills a basin and I pee.

*   *   *

Having a statue put up to you is a sure path to oblivion. If you asked any casual bystander to name the two generals and the king on the occupied plinths in Trafalgar Square, they would no doubt look blank and hurry on. Even Charles I, granted such post-mortem beauty on his high-stepping horse, only attracts a few elderly and eccentric admirers who think of him as a martyr to High Church services and the divine right of kings to govern wrong. When the plinth meetings began, I wanted, above all things, a statue of Dickens, our greatest urban novelist and celebrator of London. Dickens and poor children, I thought, would make the correct group for the plinth. And then I was frustrated to discover that he had stipulated in his will that no statue should be put up to his memory. This seems to be entirely out of character, as Dickens was one of the great show-offs of history and killed himself by performing in public, decked out in glittering chains and sumptuous waistcoats. Unfortunately, he was not possible plinth material.

Letters continued to pour in from the well-organized campaign for a statue to Women in War, figuring ATS operators of anti-aircraft guns, WRENS at sea and Land Army girls in breeches with pitchforks. Richard Cork, *The Times'* art critic, was on our committee and has an ex-WREN for a mother, and, having lived through the Blitz, I knew about women's contribution to the defeat of Hitler. Women in War was an admirable subject for a statue, as indeed was the unknown British slave.

But then we thought of the success of the small Christ and the full square when the tree with spreading roots was unveiled. We wondered if contemporary artists would be interested in an Edwardian-style, representational statue, and if we should not have some sign of our own times as a contrast to the images of nineteenth-century imperialism. Neil McGregor and Richard Cork were in favour of a rotating exhibition of British and international sculpture which would change every year, no doubt to some applause and much abuse, and which would keep the square as a centre of interest and give an annual excuse for a party. After a discussion, we all agreed to recommend that one of the subjects to be commemorated was the suffering of slaves, and that the wartime women deserved a statue in Whitehall.

We announce our decision. The press conference seems to go without protests. A lot of photographs and interviews take place in the square where now, behind Nelson, you can see across the river to the great wheel, a more beautiful object than many London statues. In the evening I'm due to have a television discussion with a young architect and an artist who has exhibited with the 'neurotic realists' and who apparently thinks it unfair on artists to have to face public exposure of their works on anything like a plinth. He will say, I'm told, that he wouldn't have anything to do with a rotating exhibition in Trafalgar Square; this may be fortunate, as his latest work consists of an arrangement of dead rats.

Being driven to Television Centre, I determine to keep calm and forget my horror of rats which originates, I believe, from a slide I had for my magic lantern when I was very young. This depicted a man sitting up in bed wearing a nightcap, with a procession of eager rats entering his open mouth. I'm also trying to sort out, or discover, the limits of art.

Ken Tynan used to talk about 'high-definition performance'. Art should be a demonstration of skill that takes your breath away, as do trapeze artists, plate-spinners, jugglers and ski jumpers. When Velásquez paints the old woman frying eggs, it's not only an arresting composition and arrangement of shapes, not just a moving tribute to hard work, old age and the satisfaction of food; the skill required to paint the texture of broken eggs, hot oil and long-lived-in skin takes your breath away. The high-definition skill of a line of Shakespeare, a Mozart concerto, a Matisse drawing or the apparently effortless singing of Billie Holliday is what leaves the audience gasping. Is that what's wrong with 'conceptual art', the fact that assembling an unmade bed or an untidy room is not difficult? Do we only want to see performances which we couldn't manage for ourselves? As I'm pushed in a wheelchair through the corridors of Television Centre, I wonder about the high-definition performance of a pile of dead rats.

The architectural expert is dark haired, friendly and pleased with the idea of a rotating exhibition on the plinth. She would like to get rid of the Indian Army generals but I have to say that there's no money available for completely refurnishing the square. The artist looks slightly cross and hostile until the interviewer asks him if he'd like to exhibit some of his work on the plinth, a question to which he was clearly expected to answer 'no'. Instead of this, his eyes light up and he confesses he'd welcome the opportunity. What he suggests is a tower of dead pigeons, higher than Nelson's column. Would this be a high-

definition   performance?   Certainly   it's
something I couldn't bear to do myself.

*   *   *

Roy Jenkins has written a piece in praise of
Tony Blair. 'A good Prime Minister and
possibly a great one,' he writes and, just in case
this might sound like an over-enthusiastic
courtier, adds, 'But you don't tip the waiter
until the meal's over.' Roy's restaurant similes
are admirable. I remember him describing Dr
Jack Cunningham, an unconvincing minister
who became the mysteriously titled 'Cabinet
Enforcer'. 'Jack Cunningham,' Roy said,
'always weminds me of a wather down-at-heel
head waiter in a distinctly second-class
westauwant, who has the job of persuading the
customers that all the best dishes are orf.'

Roy glows with the happy certainty of a life
well lived. From a mine official's house in
Wales to the great offices of State, taking time
off to produce, apparently effortlessly, a
number of heavyweight biographies of such
characters as Gladstone, Asquith, Dilke and
now Churchill, he has also enjoyed, it has been
suggested, a number of quite grand love
affairs. Florid and smiling joyfully, whilst
uttering well-constructed sentences, he opens
and shuts one hand as though pumping a small
organ to keep the whole great oratorio
flowing.

He was Chancellor of the Exchequer and probably the best Home Secretary of my lifetime. He was also President of the European Commission and, when he took on the job, chose a Mr X, MP (the name has stuck in no one's memory) to assist him. Speaking to a gathering of friends and supporters, Roy meant to say, 'I'm going into Europe without rancour.' Owing to his lifetime's avoidance of the letter 'R', the last word came out sounding suspiciously like 'wanker', whereupon one of his surprised friends said, 'Oh, really Roy? We thought you were taking Mr X with you.'

Apart from producing these occasional confusions, Roy's speeches are wonderfully shaped and strongly evocative. Once a year he turned up at the Royal Society of Literature to present the prizes we give each other to cheer ourselves up. 'It's far more agweeable,' he said, 'to give away pwizes than to wait and see if you've got one. When I was shortlisted for the Whitbwead for my *Life of Gladstone*, and didn't win, I felt as though I were a naked girl in the slave market of St Louis and Clark Gable comes up, pokes me with his umbwella and goes onto more attwactive matewial. I am left,' Roy beamed, perfectly content in his new role as a naked slave girl, 'in the Salon des Wefusées.'

He used to stay in Italy with two elegant and sometimes quarrelsome ladies, both now dead; Evangeline Bruce, whose husband has been an

American Ambassador to England, and Marietta Tree, in whose arms Adlai Stevenson died. Their house was very close to the one we rent and I asked Roy how he spent his days in Chiantishire. 'I go for a very agweeable walk up to the castle and the bus-stop. But never take the same woute twice!'

'Why not?' I was curious to know.

While still beaming happily, Roy lowered his voice to say, 'Kidnappers.'

The idea was so alarming that from then on, whenever we saw a strange car parked outside the Bar Dante or the grocer's shop in Radda, we wondered if Roy, bound and gagged, was locked up in the boot.

A literary lunch at Waterstones in Manchester. There are four speakers in some large, plastic hotel to entertain an eager audience of lunchers and potential book buyers. I am down to speak last, which is a desirable position as the audience is left with your last words ringing in their ears and, you hope, make a beeline for the table selling your stuff: Roy Jenkins, here with *Gladstone*, is third on the bill. During the preliminary drinks, he sidles up to me, beaming as always, with an urgent request.

'John, as I am Pwesident of the Woyal Society of Litewature, and you are only the Chairman, I claim the Wight to speak last at Waterstones Litewawy lunch. I'm sure you understand.'

He is right about our respective roles in the Royal Society of Literature. In the old days, he used to say that I was the Mrs Thatcher of that organization, while he was the Queen. However, I wasn't going to give up my advantageous place quite so easily.

'I think, Roy, you should ask our Chairman, the Manager of Waterstones.'

'You think that?' He looks vaguely amused. 'Vewy well,' and he pads off in the direction of the best bookseller in England, Robert Topping, whom I call Major Robert, because he was once in the army in Northern Ireland, but who is still fairly young. Then, during the consumption of the grapefruit segments, I see Roy busily engaged in bending Major Robert's ear.

With the arrival of the lamb and broccoli, Major Robert turns to me with a look of deep alarm.

'Roy says he's a Privy Councillor,' he says, 'and Privy Councillors are entitled to speak last at Waterstones Literary lunches.'

'Tell him you're the Chairman,' I advise him, 'and you decide.' Major Robert sighs, and turns to take on a tough assignment.

At the time of the strawberry flan, Roy leans towards me behind the back of Major Robert, whom he has, apparently, not persuaded, and fires off all his guns.

'John,' he says. 'When you are an O.M. and Chancellor of Oxford University, you will be able to speak last at Waterstones Litewawy lunches. But till that time comes, I claim that wight.'

'Roy,' I say. 'I think we must leave the order of speeches to Major Robert.'

Robert doesn't flinch and Roy makes an elegant and entertaining speech on Gladstone, from the third position. He bears me no sort of ill-will, and we part in the friendliest way, although I'm left with the vague feeling that I have shown some sort of disrespect for Oxford, the Privy Council and the Order of Merit.

CHAPTER TWENTY-FOUR

The trouble is that you have no idea what it's going to be like, and there is no one to tell you. I just read that drowning is not like sinking rapidly asleep in the water, but undergoing a lengthy and painful suffocation, although I don't believe that anybody knows. It can, at least sometimes, be easy. Myfanwy Piper had lunch with her daughter at Fawley Bottom, sat on the sofa, closed her eyes and, comfortably, died. She deserved such a gentle death, but there's no reason why anyone else should be so lucky.

The worst thing would be a death which is a sort of joke. When we were in the South of France one year, there were widespread forest fires, and small planes were used to scoop up water from the sea and, flying inland, dump it on the blazing pines. An innocent tourist was snorkelling harmlessly and happily watching the fish. He was scooped up by a plane, flown inland and dropped, from a great height, on to the forest fire. He became the subject of a law suit with an insurance company as no one could decide whether he had been killed by fire or water. That, with any luck, is not the way to go.

Of course it's not death but the process of dying that gives rise to *timor mortis*. A friend near death, whom I visited in hospital, described a strange dream and alarming hallucinations. The doctor had turned into a devilish figure who was seducing his patient's wife. Although my friend tried to point out that the doctor had grown a long and scaly tail, which was let out as an advertising space and had the names of various commercial products printed on it, his wife took no notice and surrendered to the devilish doctor's advances. I have had strange doctors. One who almost fainted when he had to give any of the children an injection; another, subsequently tried for some criminal offence, who ordered me to sleep with my feet higher than my head so that I, and such sleeping partners as I could find in those distant days, slid together down a slope like the west col of the Eiger. I have heard of a doctor who alleged he could change the traffic

240

lights to green by the power of thought. But I don't look forward to encountering one with a long, scaly tail, let out for advertising.

Very soon after Emily was born, Penny haemorrhaged terribly, losing a large proportion of her blood. Although told by the cleaning lady that it wasn't her 'life blood' and that it really wouldn't matter, she rang a sensible doctor, who closed his surgery and rushed her to hospital. It was hard to find a vein to receive new blood and, as she lay unconscious, she saw a blinding light and realized she was dying, an experience which caused her no terror. I'm sure this is the most reliable account of the experience; fear has gone with other accompanying pains and there is nothing to be afraid of in a great light, illuminating nothing.

*　　　*　　　*

It not only snowed in April, but it rained mercilessly from a cheerless, gunmetal sky. Gardeners say a puff of dust in April is worth a king's ransom, because you can sow seeds earlier in dry soil, but the garden was a dark sea of mud and the horses' paddock like the Somme battlefield.

But now it's the start of May and the young leaves have arrived, a sharp and brilliant green which will grow deep and dusty in August. The daffodils are finished, the bluebells are out and the ground is dry enough to plant broad beans, which are at their best when they're young and irresistible. Many of the trees and shrubs planted in my mother's and father's day have died of old age, but their magnolias and flowering cherries have come out, pink and cream clouds behind the borders. We go up to London for lunch with Muriel in Durrants Hotel, where the food is wonderfully unfashionable and reminds me of The White Elephant when I was first in love with Penny.

Muriel is on her way to New York to give a reading and she shames me. What's all this talk about bright lights and a short journey to extinction? She's written a new novel about Lord Lucan and plans a play for this year and another novel for the next. We discuss Lucan, who spent his life in gambling clubs and, they say, murdered the children's nanny under the impression she was his alienated wife. Immediately after the crime Lucan disappeared and has never been seen since.

Muriel's novel deals with his life in hiding. I tell her that years ago, one of Lucan's aristocratic friends sought me out at a party and asked, 'on behalf of a close friend', of course, if there was any time limit set on prosecutions for murder. I'm quite sure that the 'friend' was Lucan who, bunkered down in some African or South American hiding place, was anxious to know if there would come a time when he could emerge with safety. I said that no statute of limitations applied in murder cases. So Lord Lucan has remained, I feel sure, still alive in hiding, waiting to be resurrected in Muriel's sparkling prose.

She talks happily of her early days of fame in London, when she owned a racehorse and Evelyn Waugh and Graham Greene were so kind to her, and then of the hardship of packing for New York. She's also writing poetry and, having studied prosody, she says, can tell a villanelle from a ballade. Then, with her journey in mind, she searches desperately through her handbag. 'Oh bother!' she complains. 'I've got four lipsticks and no notebook!'

*   *   *

Now it's Sunday, the day of this year's picnic in the bluebell wood. Driving across the dried out horses' field we slide and skid against the scars made by tractors in the grass. The horses don't bother to look up, their lives are untroubled by any form of work. Hay is brought to them, they are regularly shod and their vet's bills paid. Their hunting days are over and they are in a sort of retirement home. Penny's hunter has a bad back and can only just trot. There is a little, hairy Shetland pony named Moonshine, the child of Pyramus and Thisbe, once owned by Peter Hall at Stratford. There's the thoroughbred Bella, who once ran away with an American TV executive and nearly killed her on the road. There is a huge animal that looks like the Trojan Horse, a friend's ex-hunter, and Rosie's old pony, named Ernie. At mealtimes they barge into each other and try to steal each other's food. Occasionally, like old men inappropriately after girls, they will frisk around the field, but it soon tires them and then they stand still among the buttercups.

We're on the way to the wood, where our tyres slide again on the soft and squashy mattress of fallen leaves. The sun is shining through the beech trees which stand, like pillars in the sea, deep in the haze of bluebells. The food and bottles, which have come in big baskets built to be slung on the backs of Moroccan donkeys, are unloaded. The dogs are jumping over the bluebells and the children are running down the hill after them. My chair, ridiculously solid, has also been carried from the car and I'm sitting on it like some absurd Canute making a drawing room of the wood and giving orders to the advancing tide of wild flowers. I feel neither old nor in any way incapacitated. Everything is perfectly all right.